An excellent time capsule for anyone who grew up in the 70s and 80s. Young Tara captures the sights, sounds and smells of life during that period while navigating complicated adult relationships, the only way a child could. It will bring you joy while making your heart heavy. A perfect story of imperfect adults doing the best they could to protect little Tara.

—Colleen Rusholme,
National Syndicated Radio Host and Television Narrator

I loved this story! It packed a punch and it was a great tie-in to "Little Girl in the Mirror". "Me and My Shadow" had a fantastic ending. Very satisfying!

—Debby Spitzig, Author of "Inspiring Birth Stories"

A heart-warming continuation of "Little Girl in the Mirror, Cathy's Story" told through the journey of Tara's childhood.

—Shannon Foley

They do say that grandchildren are grandparents' second chances, and that's evident in "Me and My Shadow".

—Lindsey-Anne Pontes,
Author of "Let Me Save You"

This is a story about relationships, difficult issues and trauma, and ultimately, about transformation through forgiveness.

—Ruth Thompson,
Author of "A Heart for Healing"

A wonderful story! I thoroughly enjoyed and was captivated by this book about a young girl and the women in her life that have their struggles and their differences but can still operate together as a family.

—Boni Batty

"Me and My Shadow" is a book that stays with you long after you've finished. I loved the unique personalities of all the characters in this story. If I can fall in love with a character as much as I did with these, those characters can literally do anything, and I'd follow them anywhere!

—Telma Rocha, Author of "The Angolan Girl",
"From Far And Wide", "Twenty-Eight Years"

This story depicted how extraordinarily beautiful simple moments in time can be. Readers are taken through Tara's emotional journey, as she learns to make sense of the world around her, and tries to bring together the people she loves best.

—Jennifer Dinsmore,
Fiction Editor and Professional Proofreader

Tara's book, "Me and My Shadow", spoke to me and gave me much insight of Tara's understanding of her mother and grandmother's relationship as seen in the mind's eye of a young girl who loved them both. If you've read "Little Girl in the Mirror", then this story is a must read!

—Brenda Schippling

Mondou shares a gut-punch of an emotional roller coaster ride, leading the reader through generational family trauma, buried family secrets, and the anxious and burning quest of a young girl trying to mend old wounds. You'll be moved and captivated by this heart-felt and poignant journey.

—Mark Leslie, Author of "Lover's Moon"

ALSO BY TARA MONDOU:

"Little Girl in the Mirror, Cathy's Story"

Me and My Shadow

Tara's Story

TARA MONDOU

"Here I am in my own house, alone with my cat Ginger. At one time I had my mother, my husband, my son, and my daughter. Now my daughter is busy with her family, my mother and my husband have passed away, and my son is in another city. Maybe something or someone will come into my life to brighten up my days; it's remaining to be seen."

— Taken from the diary of Rita Barron

"We're so close, Tara and I. I can't say how grateful I am for that. She's like having a mother, sister, daughter, and best friend rolled into one."

—Taken from the diary of Catherine Barron

For any information regarding permission contact Tara Mondou via
www.taramondou.com

Paperback ISBN 978-0-9949974-2-5
EBook ISBN 978-0-9949974-3-2

Printed in Canada

FIN 27 10 2022

Cover design: Laura Bowman

This is a work of creative nonfiction. The events and people depicted in this story are portrayed to the best of Tara Mondou's ability; inspired by a collection of letters, photographs, and memories of childhood stories. While all the stories in this book are true, they may not be entirely factual, and remain alive today only from the perspective of Catherine and Rita; who are no longer with us to tell the story themselves.

From Nana, Gramma and Mom,

to Me, Lilianne and Amelia.

Our strength carries on…

Me and My Shadow

Tara's Story

CHAPTER ONE

April 1984—Happy Easter?

"I will never darken your 'effing door again!"

Tara stood motionless on the porch, hopelessly trying to hold back tears while her mother screamed at her grandmother.

"Get in the car," her mother said through clenched teeth as she made her way past Tara then down the cracked concrete steps and away from the house.

Tara didn't know what to do: follow her mother to the car, or stay and console her grandmother? Seeing poor Gramma standing there, her face pale and her thin, trembling hand struggling to hold the screen door open, made Tara feel sick to her stomach.

What would Mom do if I hugged Gramma right now?

But, knowing her furious mother was already in the car, all Tara could do was offer a feeble smile and a weak "'Bye, Gramma…Happy Easter," before she turned and quickly headed down the steps and into the waiting car.

Before she could get her seatbelt done up, her mother smashed her foot down on the gas pedal. Spraying loose gravel, the car peeled out of the driveway as they sped toward the highway that lead back home and away from Gramma's house—forever.

Tara chose to sit in the back seat for the long drive home. She knew her mother would go silent, as she always did when she got mad. And although her mother's rage shocked Tara, she understood why her mother was so upset. As hard as Tara had tried, she couldn't get her mother and grandmother to sit down and talk about what had happened all those years ago. What had brought them both to this moment. About the thing—no, the *person*—Tara knew had been tormenting her mother since she was a little girl. Mrs. Wrenn.

Tara was only ten years old, but as far back as she could remember, her mother, Cathy, had told Tara stories about her miserable childhood growing up in the small town of Stratford, Ontario. Tara's grandmother, Rita, had given birth to Cathy in 1950, but after struggling as an unwed mother and failing to find a good job and a nice place to live, Rita had made the difficult decision to send her baby back to her parents on Cape Breton Island, Nova Scotia. Rita had begged her mother and father to take care of eighteen-month-old Cathy while she went back to Ontario to try to get her life together.

Tara knew that when her mom had been little, she'd lived happy and content in Cape Breton with her grandparents, Nana and Papa, until she was five years old. During those early years, Rita would visit Cathy for a few weeks in the summer. Then, in 1955, Rita had felt her life was stable enough that she could take Cathy back to Ontario for good. Rita swore to her parents that she would be able to take care of Cathy. She had a good job in the laundry room at the local hospital, and a nice place to live with the Gorman family.

Reluctantly, Cathy had said goodbye to Nana and Papa and everyone she'd ever known. She knew she was going to miss her grandparents and the rest of her big family in Cape Breton, but she had found herself looking forward to getting to know her mother better. Although Cathy was nervous about leaving, she'd become cautiously excited for the long train ride to Ontario and her new life with her mother.

Cathy's mother had always spoken so highly of Ontario during her annual visits to the island, but soon after Cathy arrived at the lonely train station in Stratford, her life became full of disappointments and shattered dreams.

Staring out the window as the trees and bushes along the highway rushed by, Tara remembered her mom saying that she'd been happy in Ontario for the few months they'd lived at the Gorman's, but suddenly they'd had to move out. And the only place to go was to the Wrenn's. The Wrenn family had consisted of Mr. and Mrs. Wrenn and their two adopted children, Kenny and Susan. While Cathy had lived a lonely life there, her days spent going to school and doing chores for Mrs. Wrenn, Rita had spent her days at work in the Laundry and her evenings at the Dominion Hotel— drinking, socializing, and looking for a husband.

After many long and horrible years living in the dingy upstairs room at the Wrenn's, where Mrs. Wrenn had constantly made Cathy feel nervous, scared, and unsure of herself, they'd finally moved out and into their own dusty, sparsely furnished apartment above the stationary store at 50 Wellington Street.

Cathy had thought moving into their own place, away from Mrs. Wrenn, meant she and her mother would finally have the relationship she'd always hoped for. One where Cathy would happily go to school, and afterwards they'd eat supper together and then curl up on the couch with their hot cups of tea and their books.

But Cathy's hopes of having a loving relationship with her mother were soon dashed, as Rita continued to go to the Hotel after work instead of coming home. Rita would return late, saying she was too tired to talk to Cathy before falling into the double bed they'd shared in the cramped, one-bedroom apartment.

During that year in the Wellington Street apartment, they'd lived together, day in and day out, more like roommates than family; drifting through life without ever really getting along. By the time Cathy was eleven years old, she had realized that her mother would never be the kind of mother she'd wanted, and so Cathy kept to herself and hoped for the best.

But as Cathy sunk deeper and deeper into her miserable life, she often didn't have the energy to go to school on days when she felt too sad and too lonely to try to pretend that life with her mother was OK. Life was not how she'd envisioned it back when she'd been five years old and on the train that had taken her away from Cape Breton.

After about a year, Rita had finally met a man who agreed to help take care of Cathy. Within a few months Rita and Big Joe had gotten engaged and bought an old, derelict house at 98 Railway Avenue.

Many times, Tara had asked her mom what life had been like in the new house with her mother and Big Joe, but Cathy would just press her lips firmly together and fall silent. Eventually, all she would say is that she only lived there a few short years before she'd moved out for good. By then, her mother and Big Joe had had a baby boy named Joey. Cathy fell in love with Joey, but she said that even her love for him could not keep her in "that house". When Tara asked again why her mom had moved out at such an early age, she only shook her head and said, "I just couldn't live there anymore… I had to leave."

When she was fourteen years old, Cathy had moved into an apartment with her friend. Tara had a hard time believing that two fourteen-year-old girls had been allowed to live on their own, but her mom said that that's how it was in those days. Cathy had then started dating her friend's older brother, and soon after they'd gotten engaged and moved in together. At seventeen Cathy married him, and two years later had Tara's older brother Ronnie. Then, at twenty-three, Cathy had Tara.

When Tara was about a year old—just a baby—Cathy and her husband divorced. He stayed around for a couple years, but eventually he moved to Alberta where Ronnie would visit him during the summers. Not long after, Cathy met another man, Terry, and married him. Terry had wanted to be a dad to Tara, and because of something her mom called "custody issues" with her real father, Cathy had decided that Terry could raise Tara as his own.

Tara loved her stepdad, but she knew that things weren't good between him and her mom, and things were definitely not

OK between him and her brother, Ronnie. She didn't know exactly why, but it must have had something to do with why the three of them fought all the time. When they started fighting, Tara would run up to her room and play dress-up, or pretend she was a fashion model, or make up a new dance routine. Eventually, Terry would leave the house to go to his workshop in an empty old barn he rented in the country and Tara and her mom and Ronnie would settle back into their quiet, peaceful routines.

Several years later, Cathy and Terry separated. And as soon as they did, he'd moved into an old farmhouse near his workshop at the barn. Tara still visited him on a regular basis, but he never lived in their house again.

Without Terry in his life, Ronnie was able to focus on sports and his friends but when he was home, he spent a lot of his time watching TV alone in his bedroom. And Tara spent a lot of her time talking to their mom.

She was always happy when her mom would stop cleaning or cooking for a minute so Tara could talk about movies and books, and her dolls and stuffed toys, and their pets, and her friends, and her favourite songs on the radio. Her mom would nod and listen for a few minutes, and then she would get busy again cleaning the kitchen floor or washing the dining room windows. She never said much; she was usually quiet and often didn't talk at all. Sometimes it had seemed as if her mom wanted to say something, but instead she would just raise her eyebrows and open her eyes wide. Her face said a lot—but *she* didn't. She mostly just let Tara do the talking.

Their best talking times were either on long car rides, or on Sunday mornings when Tara would crawl into her mom's bed and they'd watch *Coronation Street* on the little television set while her mom drank tea and ate toast. When her mom wasn't so preoccupied with redecorating or looking up a new recipe, Tara would ask lots of questions about Stratford and her grandmother and her mom's childhood.

And her mom would tell her all about Mrs. Wrenn. How she had been so mean to her. How she hadn't let Cathy drink her milk until after she'd eaten her whole meal. How she'd made Cathy eat Grape-Nuts, which had tasted like gravel. How she wouldn't let Cathy have any of the fresh buns that the bread man delivered on the weekends.

Tara would laugh at these stories because they hadn't seemed so terrible…at least not so bad that they would make her mom hate Mrs. Wrenn as much as she did—but if her mom hated Mrs. Wrenn, then so did she.

"Someday, when you're older, I'll tell you more about what Mrs. Wrenn did to me," her mom would say. "I lived in hell with Mrs. Wrenn, and all I had to tell my troubles to was the little girl in the mirror."

Tara knew all about the little girl in the mirror. When she was young, Cathy hadn't had any friends she could share her miserable life with, so instead, she would talk to her own reflection in any mirror she could find. Whenever Mrs. Wrenn had been especially mean, Cathy would soothe the little girl in the mirror and do her best to make her feel better.

"Did you know that Mrs. Wrenn had a stupid rule where I wasn't allowed to wear my underpants to bed?" her mom told Tara one Sunday morning. "I hated the feeling of being exposed, so I would wear them anyway. But then I would have to wake up early in the morning to take them off before Mrs. Wrenn crept up the stairs and pulled back my blankets to check. Can you imagine? What a hateful woman she was."

As many times as Tara had heard this story, she could never get over it. She just couldn't understand why Mrs. Wrenn had made such a strange rule, or why her mom had to follow it.

"Why didn't you just tell her no?" Tara would ask over and over again. "Or why didn't you tell Gramma about how Mrs. Wrenn treated you? I'm sure if you'd told Gramma, she would have packed up your things and left that house right away!"

When Tara asked these questions, her mom would just look at her and shake her head. "I did tell her, Tara, but she never listened. She just always said that Mrs. Wrenn wasn't that bad and that I should follow her rules so that we wouldn't get kicked out of the house."

This bothered Tara because she knew that if *she'd* been the one living with Mrs. Wrenn, she would have told her right off. *And* she definitely would have made sure that Gramma had listened to her and stuck up for her and made plans to move out.

Tara often wondered if her mom didn't properly remember her experiences living with Mrs. Wrenn—that maybe she was exaggerating or had misunderstood Mrs. Wrenn. Her mom had only been a young girl at that time, and Tara was sure that Gramma would have done more to help. Gramma was so sweet and kind, Tara couldn't believe she wouldn't have done something to keep her daughter safe and away from someone as awful as Mrs. Wrenn.

No matter how many times Tara questioned her mom about her stories, and no matter how many times Tara suggested that her mom ask Gramma why she hadn't taken her away from the Wrenn house, the conversation always led straight back to how horrible Mrs. Wrenn had been.

And at the end of every Mrs. Wrenn story, her mom would say, "I hated that woman until the day she died…and then I forgave her."

There were many stories over the years that led to many questions; questions Tara never really got the answers to. Sometimes Tara felt she was beginning to understand what had happened, but every time she got close, either her mom or Gramma would give her answers that didn't make sense, or clam up and change the subject altogether. Tara felt bad that they didn't get along. She loved them both very much, and wanted them to love each other too.

She glanced up at the rearview mirror and watched her mom for a moment. She still looked angry, but she also looked sad. She wished her mom would talk more about her feelings. She wished her mom would explain more about why she'd get so upset almost every time they went to Gramma's house. Although Tara felt sorry for her mom, she also felt frustrated at the whole situation.

It was one thing to feel the tension between her mom and Gramma during visits, but her mom yelling and swearing at

Gramma like she'd just done was too much. Tara knew her mom kept things bottled up, but she didn't think it was fair for her mom to treat poor Gramma that way.

It was clear that her mom hated Mrs. Wrenn, but why was she always so upset around Gramma? And why had her mom got so furious that she'd threatened to never darken Gramma's door again?

Tara wondered if she could think back to all her visits with Gramma in Stratford. If she could remember anything that would explain why her mom was always so uncomfortable around Gramma; and if she could figure out the reason behind her mom's emotional outburst before leaving just now?

As a toddler, Tara had stayed overnight with Gramma a few times. Those memories were hard to recollect, but at five years old she had started visiting Gramma for two weeks every summer. Those were vivid memories. Good memories.

Maybe she could use those memories to help her understand the two women she loved the most, and why their relationship seemed so full of sadness, distrust, and disappointment.

CHAPTER TWO

Summer 1979—Five Years Earlier

Summer vacation had finally arrived!

Tara loved playing with her friends every morning at kindergarten, and she had a lot of fun in the afternoons at her new babysitter's house, but now that school was over and the summer holidays had begun, her mom had said Tara could go for a long visit to her grandmother's house in Stratford. Her mom and stepdad had to work during the week, and like he did every summer, her brother Ronnie was going to Alberta to visit their real dad. So her mom, finally, and after a lot of consideration, agreed that Tara could go to Stratford for two whole weeks.

She remembered listening to her mom and Gramma talking on the phone a while ago about when Tara could have a summertime visit. Gramma had asked if Tara could stay at her place for two weeks, but her mom had at first said no; that was too long and Tara was too young. Tara had wanted so badly to spend two weeks with Gramma. She loved her very much and they always had a lot of fun because Gramma told funny stories, sang Irish songs, and let Tara stay up late to watch whatever she wanted on TV.

When Tara had begged her mom to let her go, she had said, "Tara, I know you love Gramma and have fun when you're there, but two weeks is a long time. I'll be worried that you're not eating properly or getting enough sleep, or not having regular baths and getting your hair washed. Will Gramma know if you're feeling sick, or missing me, or wanting to come home? Will she listen to you and pay attention to you?"

"Gramma always pays attention to me and she listens to me and takes care of me. Please, please can I go?"

Her mom had pressed her lips together and looked directly into Tara's eyes. "We'll see," was all she'd said.

But now, a few weeks later, her mom said she'd thought long and hard, and even though she was nervous to let Tara go to Stratford for so long, she'd decided that they could try it this one time and see how it went.

Tara didn't know what her mom was nervous about, or why she was worried that Gramma wouldn't take care of her, but she was so excited that she'd been allowed to go she didn't ask any questions that might change her mom's mind.

"OK, little girl! Your big day is finally here," her mom said as she put Tara's suitcase in the trunk of their car. "And it's a beautiful, sunny day, so we'll be able to drive with the windows down."

"How long will it take to get there, Mommy?" Tara asked as she put on her seatbelt and got comfortable in the back seat.

"We'll be there in about half an hour." Her mom looked at her watch. "But we better get crackin' so we're not late."

As her mom backed the car down the driveway, she asked, "What do you think? Do you want to go on the highway or on the back roads?"

"Let's take the back roads!" answered Tara, excited to head out on the old country roads that would take them all the way to Gramma's house.

Her mom smiled into the rearview mirror, pulled out onto the busy road, and stepped on the gas. She tuned the radio until she found one of her favourite songs, then started singing out loud. She rolled down the windows and a rush of warm summer air blew their hair all over the place, making them laugh as they sang.

Taking the back roads meant driving fast along the rolling yellow-and-green farmers' fields, and speeding past big, old houses and colourful barns; some red with white trim and some dark green with black trim. There were lots of barnyard animals to watch out for, and some to smell too! There were pigs playing in their manure piles, and chickens running around the yard and pecking at unknown things in the ground, but Tara kept her eyes peeled for the beautiful brown horses who were casually waiting for her to wave from the speeding car. After greeting the horses, Tara knew the black-and-white cows would soon come into view and she waited, knowing what her mom would do next.

"Moooooo," said her mom in a slow, low voice. "MOOOOOOO!"

"Mommy, you sound just like a cow!" Tara laughed.

"I know, that's why I do it." Her mom grinned. "They think I'm their mother."

Their car zoomed past a small graveyard perched on top of a grassy hill. Her mom squinted at Tara in the rearview mirror, and sounding serious asked, "How many people do you think are dead in that graveyard?"

With a knowing smile, Tara answered. "All of them!"

"Thank God!" Her mom laughed, turning up the volume on the radio.

When they got to the other side of a small town called Shakespeare, which Tara knew was about ten minutes away from Gramma's house, her mom stopped being silly. She pressed her lips tightly together, turned the radio down, and drove a bit slower. She didn't say anything more as they made their way through town—up Ontario Street, across Romeo toward Downie, and through the quiet, tree-lined streets that led to 98 Railway Avenue.

The street was perfectly named because the two-story, mustard-yellow brick house was only about ten feet away from the railway tracks. Directly behind the small garden that Gramma's husband, Big Joe, kept in the back of the house, was a steep embankment with railway tracks laid out on the very top. Big, heavy freight trains and sleek, shiny passenger trains rolled by several times a day. Passenger trains leaving the Stratford station were pretty quiet until they geared up and headed west toward London. But if they came *in* from the west, they would barrel down the tracks, their brakes shrieking as they worked hard to slow down before arriving at the station. When freight trains pulled out of the station, the sound of their groaning engines and lumbering steel wheels, along with sudden blasts from the horn to warn people off the tracks, was enough to make Tara jump out of her skin. If she heard it in the distance as it gained momentum, she could brace herself for the horrendous sound, but if she was preoccupied with the TV or looking at picture albums or something, the rumbling of the engine and the shaking of the house, would give her such a fright she felt sure she would have a heart attack.

Whenever Tara would talk to her mom about the trains that passed back and forth behind Gramma's house, her mom would tell stories about the first time she'd taken the train all the way from Nova Scotia to Ontario. Tara often daydreamed about how her mom must have felt when her whole life had changed; and not just where she lived, but how she'd gone from being surrounded by family in the small house on Woodward Street to the lonely room she'd shared with her mother at Mrs. Wrenn's house. She knew that as a little girl her mom had always dreamed of the day that she could leave her miserable life with the Wrenns and take the same train back to Nana and Papa and live with them instead.

"OK, we're here," her mom said as she turned into the driveway. She eased the car to a stop before the gravel gave way to the long grass growing at the side of the house. "Oh look, she's already waiting at the door."

Tara forgot about the trains, and her mom's life as a little girl, and looked up to see her grandmother standing in the doorway holding the screen door wide open to welcome them inside. Tara jumped out of the car and ran up the four cracked concrete steps to the porch.

"Hi, Gramma, we're here!" Tara said as she gave her grandmother a quick hug, then bent down to pet Smokey, Gramma's thirty-pound black cat. "It didn't take us long, did it?"

"No, it didn't. You two got here lickety-split," Gramma said with a big smile. "And my goodness, Tara, you're growing like a weed!"

"Hi, Mom." Her mom carried Tara's small suitcase up the steps, past her mother and daughter, and into the front hall. "I'm not staying long."

"Well, surely you can stay for a hot cup of tea before you go?" Gramma said as she shooed Smokey down the steps to go hunt mice in the long grass.

"Alright, a quick one then. Is the kettle on?" Her mom walked into the kitchen and glanced at the stove. The water was already boiling, and she reached up to the tin on the shelf and fished out two bags of Red Rose.

From what Tara could remember about being at Gramma's; there was always someone dying for a hot cup of tea—just like at her house in Kitchener when her Aunt Marlene would come over. There was always a whistling kettle, tea-stained cups, and cold squished teabags on the side of the sink.

"The Carnation's in the fridge, hun," Gramma said as she took her cigarette pack out of her apron pocket and settled herself at the kitchen table to light one.

"I know where the Carnation is, Mom." Her mom pressed her lips together and poured hot water over the teabags.

"Where's Big Joe?" Tara asked as she moved the cigarette-making machine and the tin of tobacco away from her place at the kitchen table. She knew that as soon as Big Joe came home he would let her make cigarettes for him and Gramma—it was one of her favourite jobs!

"Oh, he'll be walking through that door any minute now, dear," answered Gramma, exhaling smoke toward the open window. "Poor Joe will be happy to be off for the weekend. He's been working so hard at St. Mary's Cement, and with that heart attack he took last winter he's been very tired by the end of the week…but he's really looking forward to seeing you, Tara, and to watching you sing and dance in the pantry the way you do."

"Alright, I should get going," her mom said suddenly, putting her half-empty tea cup in the sink with all the other dirty dishes. "I need to get back home to let the dogs out."

"Hun, you just got here. Do you have to go already?" asked Gramma, butting out her cigarette before following her daughter to the front door.

Her mom grabbed her purse off the wooden bench in the front hall and gave Tara a big hug and kissed her cheek. "OK, little girl, you have fun and I'll see you in two weeks." She headed out the door and down the crumbling steps. "Bye, Mom," she said over her shoulder.

Tara stood on the porch and watched her mom back out of the driveway. She stuck her hand out of the window to wave goodbye, and Tara waved back until she couldn't see the car any longer. Even though Tara knew she was a big girl now, and knew she would have fun with Gramma, she couldn't help but feel a little anxious at seeing her mother's car disappear down the road.

Tara suddenly wondered if she was going to miss her mom too much to stay in Stratford for two weeks—she had never been away from her for so long before. But when she saw Smokey bound up the steps with a dead mouse flopping in his mouth, she laughed and realized just how excited she was to spend so much time with her grandparents.

———————◆◄∞►•———————

Tara was in the living room taking her things out of her suitcase, and Gramma was busy in the kitchen, draining the potato water into the sink, when she heard her grandfather holler from the front door in his thick Polish accent.

"Hello, I home! Who is here?"

"It's me, Big Joe!" Tara answered as she jumped up from the living room floor and ran into the front hall to greet him. "Did you know I was here?"

"Well, I don't know much about you, or where you be, but look inside here, OK?" he said, gesturing to the big grey lunchbox sitting on the wooden bench. "Something for you, I think."

With a knowing smile, Tara opened the lunchbox and there inside, wrapped in wax paper, were two ginger cookies. Tara knew Big Joe didn't eat his cookies on the days she came to visit. She took a bite and thought about her grandfather as she watched him take off his work boots.

Big Joe wasn't someone who talked much, and with the scowl he often wore you would think he was grumpy all the time. He was short, with a big belly and barely enough grey hairs to comb across his head. His cheeks were almost always red, but his eyes were the brightest blue Tara had even seen.

Gramma had told Tara that, when Big Joe was a young man, he'd been in the war against Germany, and because he was Polish, bad things had happened to him. Tara now wondered if that's why he sometimes yelled really loud, or why his blue eyes flashed if something made him mad. Luckily, Tara didn't see that side of him very often. Most of the time he was at work, and when he came home he spoke in a quiet voice.

"You being good girl?" he asked. But before Tara could answer, he patted her on the head and went to lie down on the couch to rest.

After an early supper of cabbage, roast beef, and carrots, Big Joe went to the backyard to tend his garden, and Tara and Gramma made themselves comfortable in the two worn lawn chairs out on the front porch. (Well, Tara called it a porch, but Gramma always referred to it as the veranda.) Gramma had gotten herself a cold bottle of beer, and a glass of lemonade for Tara, and as usual she wore her apron, her cigarettes in one pocket and her lighter and a wad of tissue in the other.

It was the perfect summer evening to be outdoors; up and down Railway Avenue, the neighbours sat in the shade of their own verandas as kids in shorts and T-shirts played with a ball in the street and couples walked hand-in-hand down the sidewalk.

Gramma lit a cigarette and slowly exhaled as she gazed across the street.

"Who is that man, Gramma?" Tara asked, following Gramma's gaze and pointing to the shadowy porch where an older man quietly smoked his own cigarette.

"Oh, that's just Walter, dear," Gramma answered as she sat up, straightening her white blouse and smoothing her wavy black hair. "He's Polish, like Big Joe."

She sat back again and looked at Tara. "You know, it's comical. When your mommy was young, she used to call him Walter *Glass Whiskey*. His last name is actually Glaszewski, but she could never say it right."

"Mommy knew him when she was a little girl?" asked Tara. "That was a long time ago, right Gramma?"

"Yes, it was a long time ago. I knew Walter before I met my Joe, but I don't really know him anymore," Gramma said as she leaned over to pick up her half-empty beer bottle.

"During the summer when your mommy and I lived on Wellington Street, my sister, Joanie, and her husband Stan—do you remember meeting them?—well, they invited me on a double date with a man Stan worked with. His name was Joe. We had a lovely time that night, and we started dating right away. We got engaged within a few months and were married at St. Joseph's Catholic Church that December. Once we were married, Joe bought this house and Cathy and I moved in after Christmas. And you know what? As soon as I met him I knew he was the man I wanted to marry, and nothing made me happier than knowing Joe was going to take care of my Cathy-O."

"So how did Mommy know Walter Glass Whiskey?" Tara asked as she watched the man slowly raise his hand and wave.

Gramma quickly returned the wave before standing up and turning her back on the man across the street. She put her cigarette out in the ashtray and said, "That was a long time ago, dear. Let's go inside and get you ready for bed."

As Tara stood up to follow Gramma into the cool, quiet house, she tried remembering her mom ever telling her about Walter Glass Whiskey. Thinking about Walter also made Tara think about her mom's father and who he was. Many times, Tara had asked her mom who her father was: what was his name, where was he, and why didn't they ever visit him? Her mom said she didn't have a lot of information, but she knew her father's name was Reg Larion; that he was the brother of Aunt Kay's husband, Frank; that he never married Gramma, that he married someone else and lived in a city called Brantford. He and his wife didn't have any other children.

Her mom had also said that Uncle Frank was kind to her and helped Gramma whenever he could, but his brother, Reg, had never acknowledged that he was her father. Once her mom had realized that Reg didn't want her, she'd decided that she didn't want him either. So she'd tried her best to just forget about him.

Tara felt bad that her mom hadn't had a dad to love her, and she felt sad for Gramma that Reg hadn't wanted to marry her. Maybe, during the next two weeks, she would ask Gramma about Reg Larion and find out more about him and why he didn't want to be her mom's father

CHAPTER THREE

Summer 1979—Gramma's House

"I'll go up and get the sheets and blankets to make up your bed, dear," Gramma said as she started up the creaky stairs, heading to the small room where she kept her extra things. "You just stay down here. I'll be back in a jiffy."

Tara sat on the bench in the front hall, and as she was waiting for Gramma to come back down, she realized that Gramma's house wasn't big—but it wasn't small either. The biggest piece of furniture was Gramma's old buffet, which was in the front hall and was the first thing you saw as soon as you came in the door. Stuffed in the drawers, and in the space below, she kept all her photo albums, various pieces of used wrapping paper, brown paper bags from the grocery store they called the A&P, and anything else that could fit. Opposite the buffet was a pretty wooden bench, the one she sat on now, that had a lid that opened up and inside Gramma kept a few toys for kids to play with; a baseball and a glove, a pair of metal roller skates, and Tara's favourite, a plastic bowling ball and a set of brightly coloured plastic pins. Mounted on the wall above the bench was the big black telephone that Gramma spent many hours on, smoking cigarettes and talking to her friends and family.

To the left of the front hall was a flight of stairs to the second floor, where there were three bedrooms: her grandparents', her Uncle Joey's, and the room Nana used when she visited. There was also a bathroom, and a small room tucked in between Nana's bedroom and the stairwell. This small room was the one that Tara called the "attic room" because it was the only room in the house that had access to the actual attic, that dark, scary space at the top of the house. In the attic room, Gramma kept a wardrobe full of extra clothes and blankets, boxes piled high with things she'd collected over the years, and an old metal cot that was folded up and stored under the dusty window. On the far side of the attic room, a small door opened up to a steep flight of stairs.

Once, when she'd felt especially brave, Tara had opened the door. But after looking up those creepy stairs that disappeared into the darkness, she'd lost the nerve to go any further. Besides, there was no need to go up there because she was pretty sure that was where the monsters lived. Better to just leave them alone.

Downstairs, from the front hall, you could go straight through to the kitchen and to the pantry at the far end of the house. From the right of the hallway, you could go into the large living room that was divided into two areas. In the front area was an arched window that overlooked the street, and beside it sat a large floor model TV with dusty, framed pictures littered across the top. Most of Gramma's furniture was scratched and damaged, so she covered every inch in the doilies that her sister-in-law Elsie crocheted and gave her on special occasions. Against one wall was a big and worn, but comfortable, chair, and beside it sat Gramma's blanket-covered armchair, which was positioned right behind her much-needed footstool. Under the many couches, chairs, tables, and floor lamps lay a matted, dark-green carpet. If Tara looked closely, she could see black cigarette burn holes scattered here and there.

On the opposite wall from Gramma's chair was the long, comfortable couch that Tara used as a bed ever since she'd gotten too big to sleep in Gramma's room. One time, Gramma had asked Tara if, instead of sleeping on the couch, she would maybe rather sleep on the metal cot in the small room upstairs? Tara's eyes had grown wide and she'd shook her head from side to side. "The attic room? Oh, no, no!" And so, from the time Tara had been only three or four years old, she'd slept alone in the living room on her very own couch.

In the back part of the living room was another large window hung with heavy, gold-coloured curtains, and beneath it another couch where Big Joe took his naps. The window looked out over the small back garden and the train tracks beyond. Against the side wall was the antique china cabinet where Gramma kept her pretty ballerina figurines and the miniature ceramic statues she'd collected from Red Rose tea boxes. Against the wall leading to the kitchen was a large, chest-like record player, with Gramma's favourite Harry Hibbs and Nana Mouskouri records stored in the cabinets attached to the sides. Beside the record player was a rocking chair covered in an old blanket. Nana's chair.

Nana was Gramma's mother, and she had been living with Gramma and Big Joe until just a few months ago. But when Big Joe took his heart attack, Nana had decided to go back to Cape Breton to live with her daughter Big Molly, and her family.

Tara had been sad when she found out that Nana had gone back to Cape Breton. She'd loved going to Gramma's knowing that Nana would be there. Nana slept upstairs, in the bright, sunny room between the attic room and the bathroom. She had a single bed with a white headboard, and a small dresser with what she called a "tri-fold" mirror on top. Whenever Tara would visit Nana in her room, Nana would say, "Look in there, my dear, in the top drawer of the dresser." Deep inside the drawer would be a pile of clean tissue with white mints sitting on top. "Take a couple," she'd whisper, "and put them in your pocket for later, but don't tell anyone where you got them."

Nana's real name was Catherine Barron. Nana's children called her Mama, but her grandchildren—and great-grandchildren—called her Nana. Tara knew that her mom had been named after Nana, but instead of calling her Catherine, Gramma always called her Cathy.

Nana was really old. She had wavy white hair, thick glasses, a large curved nose, and a pointy chin. She almost never wore outside clothes or shoes—she would just layer herself in two or three housedresses and wear an old pair of fluffy slippers. She was tall, and had big hands and feet. She was not like Gramma at all, who had small bones and dainty features and was only just over five feet tall.

While at Gramma's, Nana spent most of her days rocking in her chair at the back of the living room, reading her prayers or *The Beacon Herald*, Stratford's newspaper. She was always saying she was hard-of-hearing, and if she didn't know what you were saying, she'd stop rocking, open her brown eyes wide, and just stare at you like an owl. "What's that, my dear?" she'd ask. And before you could repeat yourself, she would reply—just as if she'd heard you in the first place.

One time, when Tara had been on her couch in the front part of the living room and watching TV and Nana had been rocking away and reading her prayer book in the back part, Tara had noticed that the creaking of the chair had stopped. She looked back to see if Nana had fallen asleep, but Nana sat perfectly still, her eyes wide open staring at Tara through the thick lenses of her glasses. A bit concerned, Tara had moved to the end of the couch to get a closer look at her great-grandmother, and suddenly she realized that Nana had pushed her dentures out of her mouth and was somehow balancing them on the end of her pointy chin! Once Nana knew for sure she had Tara's attention, she slowly sucked her teeth back in, and with a twitch at the side of her mouth, started rocking again.

Nana did a lot of silly things like that, but she never laughed and she rarely changed her stony expression. Tara's mom used to say that Nana was "deadpan," but once Tara got used to Nana and her comical ways, she'd just laugh and shake her head and turn back to what she'd been doing before.

"Here we go, dear, let's make up the sofa now so you can get ready for bed," said Gramma, interrupting Tara's thoughts as she came down the stairs with a pile of blankets.

As Tara helped Gramma finish setting up her bed on the couch, a heavy freight train made its low and rumbling way down the tracks. Tara jumped onto the couch and pulled the blanket over her head, trying to keep the horrible sound out of her ears.

Gramma gently pulled the blanket off Tara's head, and putting her thin arm around Tara's bony shoulders, she said, "I remember when you were only three years old, Tara. It was the first time you heard the freight train coming down the tracks. You ran clear across the room and jumped onto Big Joe's sofa to look out the window. You were so frightened, your eyes were as big as saucers! But I sat with you and told you not to be scared; it's only the freight train heading toward London, after all. Soon you grew so used to the sound you forgot there were train tracks running through the backyard."

Tara remembered those early visits at Gramma's, when she'd been really little. For her first sleepover, Gramma and Big Joe had set up a playpen at the end of their bed because Joey, who had been fifteen years old at the time, was in his bedroom and Nana was in her bedroom. Gramma had thought Tara was probably small enough to fit in the playpen, and at first Tara had thought it would be fun to pretend that she was still a baby. She'd fallen asleep right away, but in the middle of the night she'd woken up feeling too squished, and so she'd crawled into bed between her grandparents for the rest of the night. The next morning, Big Joe said that Tara had kicked him in the back all night, and that while she was visiting he would sleep down in the back part of the living room on his couch. Tara had loved that idea because then she could stay with Gramma all night long!

Another time, when she was a bit older, Tara had been helping Gramma put her laundry away. Gramma's room was small and dim, with only one small window that was always open—winter, spring, summer, and fall. Gramma had said that she needed fresh air at all times, and that she couldn't breathe without it. Plus, she loved to hear the birds chirping during the spring.

"Did you know that there is a bird who lives in a tree just outside the window that calls to me every morning? He says, 'Rita, Rita, Rita,' over and over again until I wake up. He's my little alarm clock!"

Gramma had a double bed with a dark yellow bedspread, a headboard with a cupboard where she kept a glass bowl full of holy water and an overflowing ashtray. On either side of the bed was an old wooden chair. There wasn't much closet space, so most of Gramma's and Big Joe's clothes were draped over the backs of these chairs. The piles of clothes were so high that Tara was sure the items on the bottom layer had never seen the light of day.

Gramma was very religious. Well, not as religious as Nana, but pretty religious. She blessed herself with the holy water two times a day, and she never missed her morning or her evening prayers. She was always digging out the rosary and her prayer books that she kept in the cupboard above her bed.

"What's in there, Gramma?" Tara had asked while folding a towel. "Behind that closed door."

"Why that's the clothes closet, dear." Gramma had opened the door and moved the hanging items aside so Tara could take a look. "See?"

Tara had been surprised to see so many pretty things hanging inside: a beautiful dark-green dress, another slippery-looking dress with big blue flowers, and, on the floor bunched up in a ball, a bright-pink bathing suit. Tara couldn't picture her grandmother in any of those fancy clothes because normally all Gramma wore were dark polyester slacks with either a white sleeveless blouse or a snug-fitting, pale-coloured, long-sleeved sweater. In the house, on account of her sore feet from when she worked in the laundry at the hospital, and later when she worked at a factory called Blackstone, she always wore black leather shoes with thick white socks. Gramma had always told stories of how much she'd liked working behind the counter at a store called Comley's, but said whatever work she'd done in the past, being on her feet now-a-days hurt too much. So she stayed at home and babysat the neighbour's grandkids.

The last item in the bedroom was an old antique dresser with a large oval mirror suspended between two curved wooden arms. The glass in the mirror was dark and pitted, and as with the other furniture in the house the dresser top was scratched and damaged, and so it was covered with one of Aunt Elsie's doilies. Scattered on top of the yellowed doily were several bottles of creams and perfumes, framed pictures of family members, a small jewellery box, and a large statue of the Virgin Mary.

When Tara was alone in Gramma's bedroom, she liked to look in the mirror and pretend she was a movie star. She would go through Gramma's limited amount of makeup: dark-pink rouge, light-pink lipstick, and loose face powder that you put on with a big fluffy puffball. She would comb her straight, light-brown hair with Gramma's brush and pretend she was getting ready for her big performance on the stage. The "stage" was set up in the pantry just off the kitchen, and putting on shows for Gramma and Big Joe was one of her favourite things to do.

"You look beautiful, Tara!" Gramma would say when she'd find Tara up in her bedroom. "Try some of that perfume I got for Christmas. It's called White Shoulders, and is it ever nice."

Tara loved the smell of White Shoulders, and she thought the bottle with the lady on the front was so pretty. She'd put a dab behind her ears and ask, "How does that smell, Gramma?"

"Oh, just lovely, dear," Gramma would say as she leaned in and inhaled softly. She'd then sit on the edge of the bed to light a cigarette. "You know, your mommy used to just love looking in that very same mirror. When we moved into the apartment on Wellington Street, the lady who'd lived there before us said that we could have the dresser because she didn't have anyone to help her bring it down the stairs. Sometimes, when I would come home after work, I would hear your mom talking to the mirror, telling her reflection about her day and about how she missed Nana and Papa back in Cape Breton. But whenever Cathy noticed I was in the room she would quickly say goodbye to her friend. I don't think she wanted me to know what they were talking about. Anyway, I knew your mommy loved that mirror, so I made sure that Big Joe got it moved here to this house and I've kept it ever since."

"Gramma, I love this mirror! Do you think that, when I'm older, you can give it to me?"

"That's a deal, my dear!" Gramma promised. "I will keep it safe for you so you can have it when you grow up."

"Alright, you! Let's get going or you're never going to get to bed," said Gramma now, startling Tara out of her memories. "Up we go to get you changed into your nighty and get your teeth washed."

Tara followed Gramma through the darkened front hall and up the creaky stairs to the bathroom on the second floor.

"Can we put the hall light on, Gramma? I don't like the dark."

"Of course, dear, but you have nothing to be afraid of," Gramma said as she reached up to turn on the light.

It was chilly in the bathroom because, like in Gramma's bedroom, the window was always open a crack. When the wind blew, the window casing would shake and shudder, and would make Tara feel like shutting out the night air. And there was another outside noise that Tara always wondered about. It was a sort of mechanical sound that sounded like work being done somewhere.

"Oh, that's just the sound of Standard Products over across the tracks," Gramma said when Tara asked about the strange noise. "They make rubber and plastic parts for cars and things like that. I think they work all night long, but you don't need to worry about that noise, dear. You'll get used to it. Now, you get your teeth washed and I'll be downstairs watching TV with Big Joe."

Tara loved Gramma's house and almost always felt comfortable and safe there, but she really didn't like being upstairs by herself—especially now that Nana was gone to Cape Breton and Joey was out with his friends.

After she got her nighty on and *brushed* her teeth—she smiled to herself because Gramma said to *wash* her teeth—the last thing she had to do was use the toilet. As she perched on the seat, she could feel the wind hissing though the slightly opened window and could hear the heavy push, press, sigh sounds floating in from across the tracks. She got goose bumps, and with a shudder pulled down her nighty and flushed the toilet. Gramma always told her that she had to press and hold the lever down. If it wasn't held down long enough, the toilet wouldn't flush properly. Tara hated this part, because she knew, beyond a shadow of a doubt, that the sound of the flushing toilet would wake up the monsters that lived in the top of the house.

"Hurry, hurry, hurry," she whispered as she willed the toilet water to finish swirling around the bowl.

Finally, it was done! Feeling sweaty and clammy at the same time, Tara sprinted across the bathroom and through the hall, knowing that she only had a matter of seconds before the monsters made their way down the steep steps from the top of house and into the attic room. Halfway to safety, at the top of the stairs, Tara stopped cold, her heart beating like a trip hammer. The hall light was off! The stairs that were supposed to bring her to safety disappeared into darkness.

"Gramma must have forgotten that I need the light and turned it off again when she went downstairs," Tara said to herself. "Oh my God, the monsters are coming and it's dark down there!"

She could hear shuffling movements coming from the attic room and knew it was now or never. Using all she'd learned about leaping and jumping from dance class, she grabbed the railings and hurtled herself down the stairwell and onto the landing. Then, as fast as her little legs could carry her, she tripped and stumbled down the rest of the steps until she finally reached the bottom.

She stopped, looked at herself in the big mirror that hung on the wall at the bottom of the stairs, and pushing her hair out of her face straightened her nighty and walked calmly into the living room where her grandparents were quietly watching TV.

"Hello, dear," said Gramma from her chair. "See, there's nothing to be afraid of. Now get comfortable on the sofa and we'll see what's on TV."

Behind her, Tara didn't notice as Smokey the cat made his way from his hiding spot in the attic room and down the stairs. Swishing his tail as he walked past, he sauntered his way into the kitchen and toward his often-visited and much-loved food dish.

CHAPTER FOUR

Summer 1979—Saturday at Gramma's House

Waking up on Saturday mornings at Gramma's house was the best!

Tara was allowed to sleep in until whenever she wanted, and she could take her time waking up while the heaviness of sleep slowly left her body. As she lay on her couch under the warm covers, she listened to the quiet morning sounds of the house. She could hear faint, tinny music playing from the old radio that lived on the kitchen table; Gramma's and Big Joe's hushed voices talking about the weather and how it would affect the garden tomatoes; and the slightly sickening sound of Smokey licking and smacking his wet cat food as if he hadn't eaten in days. She could smell the familiar scent of cigarette smoke and greasy fried bacon as it collided with the fresh summer breeze coming in through the open window.

She could envision Gramma sitting at the table in her thin floral nightgown and even thinner faded housecoat, her baby-blue socks pulled over her skinny white ankles, and her blue-veined legs crossed while pouring over what she called her writing tablet, scratching down grocery items to buy at the

A&P. Big Joe would be slowly smoking a cigarette, his blue eyes squinting as the smoke curled up over his face and out the open window, listening to the news while at the same time glancing down at the headlines in *The Beacon*.

Tara scurried to the end of the sofa—Gramma always called it a sofa—and popped her head around the doorway so she could see for herself if she'd been right about how she'd pictured their Saturday-morning routine.

"What do you want for supper tonight, Joe?" Gramma asked her husband, taking a sip of her hot tea.

"Whatever, Rita, I no care," answered Big Joe as he gestured for her to be quiet while he listened to the news.

Gramma jotted down a few more items. Glancing up from her tablet, she spied Tara peeking out from the living room. "Oh, would you look at that, Joe? There's a little girl watching you!"

"Good morning. I'm awake now," said Tara as she kicked off her blankets, jumped off the couch, and made her way into the kitchen.

"You hungry?" Big Joe asked. "Rita, get her eggs…she hungry."

"Now you sit right there at your spot, dear, and I'll fix you your breakfast. Big Joe left a few slices of bacon for you, and I'll get you your egg."

"Can I get the egg timer?" Tara asked as she rummaged through the cupboard beside the stove, looking for the red wooden timer.

"Of course, dear. Now, hop up on your chair and I'll tell you when you can turn it over."

After all the sand had sifted through the hourglass, Gramma popped the egg out of the hot water and into its holder. Tara loved when Gramma put the egg in its cute plastic cup. It was easy for her to carefully tap the top off and dip her long strips of toast into the warm yolk. Gramma always knew how she liked her eggs: soft-boiled to perfection!

Tara finished her breakfast and since Big Joe and Gramma were still comfortable at the kitchen table, she asked if she could turn off the radio. "Of course, dear. Why? What are you up to?"

"I would like you to now pay close attention, because Miss Tara will be performing her famous song and dance just for you!" Tara bellowed in her best ringmaster voice as she jumped up and headed toward the pantry.

On Sunday afternoons past, Tara and Gramma watched all the old black-and-white movies. Their favourites always starred Judy Garland or Fred Astaire, so when she performed her song-and-dance routine, she would often make-believe she was wearing a black tuxedo, a shiny pair of shoes with white spats, and a satin top hat with a ribbon wrapped around it. To add to her costume, she'd find the long metal stick that Gramma called a "threshold". Apparently it was supposed to be screwed to the floor between the kitchen and the pantry, but it had never been installed so Tara used it as her cane.

"Please get settled and dim the lights as your talented dancer makes her way to the spotlight to sing one of her favourite tunes!" Normally, Tara would sing "By the Light of the Silvery Moon" by Bing Crosby, but for this morning's show, she decided to sing and dance to "Me and My Shadow". Just the way their favourite actress, Judy Garland, would sing it.

Big Joe laughed and Gramma clapped, and then a hush fell over the audience as they put out their cigarettes in silent anticipation.

Tara positioned herself behind the wall that separated the kitchen from the pantry. She picked up her "cane" and, as the music started in her head, she thought of all the dance moves and their funny names that her dance teacher had taught her. She said them to herself as she began her routine. *Five, six, seven, eight, kick the right leg!* She started to sing, "Me and My Shadow" *Kick the left leg.* She popped out from behind the pantry wall and into the kitchen. *Step, together, step. Hitchy-koo ball change, hitchy-koo ball change. Step-hop chasse, step-hop chasse.*

After many rounds of applause, cheers, and whistles from the crowd, she continued her carefully choreographed number and ended strong with a grand jete across the floor.

"Bravo, bravo!" Gramma yelled while Big Joe clapped.

Tara took a bow and another and then slowly backed into the pantry and behind the wall, where she waited to see if the crowd would demand an encore.

"Now that you're done your grand performance, Miss Tara, why don't you take your orange juice into the living room and I'll put the cartoons on for you," Gramma said as she filled up the sink to do the dishes, still laughing.

Although Tara would have liked to do another number, she thought it was neat that Gramma would let her have her orange juice in the living room while she sat on the couch to watch TV.

She would sing and dance again later, but for now she was happy that she was allowed to watch cartoons all morning and no one would tell her to turn the TV down, or to fold the couch blankets, or to get dressed.

"Can you come and watch Bugs Bunny with me, Gramma?" Tara could always count on Gramma to watch TV with her. They'd spent many hours together watching soap operas during the week, and late-night shows on Friday and Saturday nights when she'd slept over on weekends.

Gramma came in and sat down, putting her feet up on the stool and lighting a cigarette as Tara heard Joey coming down the stairs. He must have come home late after a night out with his friends. She wondered if he was afraid of the monster in the attic room, too, because it sounded like a herd of elephants was coming down the wooden stairs.

"Hey, Mom," said Joey as he rubbed his eyes and looked over at Tara.

"Hi, hun. I didn't hear you come in last night," Gramma said as she quickly got up from her chair. "Do you want some breakfast?"

Joey grabbed the *TV Guide* from the arm of Tara's couch and gestured his mom out of the way. "Yeah, and can you hurry because I have to get to work by ten o'clock," he said as he flicked the cartoons over to sports and then plunked himself down into Gramma's chair.

Tara hated when he did that. Didn't he know that she and Gramma were already watching something? Didn't he know that Gramma hated watching sports?

With a sigh, Tara got up, grabbed her small pile of clothes, and went upstairs to the bathroom to get dressed and ready for the day. Once in her shorts and T-shirt, she decided to go down the hall and peek into Joey's room.

The first thing she noticed was that instead of a doorknob, there was only a hole about the size of a quarter. There was no latch or anything to keep the door shut all the way. Tara was nervous to put her finger in the hole, so she just gently pushed the door open. Inside, the room was small and stuffy. There was no carpet, just roughly cut linoleum that curled up along the bottom of the stained, wood-panelled walls. Near the top of the walls, below the cracked ceiling, there was a narrow shelf where every square inch was covered in empty bottles. Tara hadn't known her uncle collected empty glass bottles, but they were the only decoration in the room. At the end of the single bed there was a small dresser with drawers that didn't quite shut, and an old nightstand beside the bed was piled high with books and magazines. On top was an overflowing ashtray and a lighter.

On the back wall, behind a set of dusty-looking curtains, was a window. Tara thought maybe she could try to open it to get some fresh air into the room, but when she went to pull the white-and-pale-blue curtains back she realized they were made of paper. How curious! All the curtains at home were made of thick, soft fabric, but these paper curtains were crinkly and frail and she was worried she would rip them if she pulled on them too hard. She decided to forget about opening the window and made her way down the stairs to the living room before Joey caught her poking around in his room.

When Tara got back downstairs, Joey was nowhere to be seen and the TV was turned off. Looking at the big black screen felt weird because it was only a very rare occasion that it wasn't on. Tara knew that Gramma must have marched right over to the TV and punched the power button off as soon as Joey left... anything to get rid of the sound of those stupid sports.

"C'mon in here, dear, and drink this tea I made you before it turns stone cold," Gramma said, calling from the kitchen. Tara looked longingly at the TV and wished she could watch more cartoons, but she made her way to the kitchen table and her cup of tea.

Before she could take a sip the phone rang and Gramma went to the front hall to answer. Tara followed her, curious to see who was calling.

"Oh, hi, hun!" Gramma said. "How are ya? Yes, she's right here...hang on. Tara, it's for you...it's your mom."

"Hi, Mommy!" Tara carefully held the heavy telephone. "I'm having a good time!"

"Hi, little girl! I'm glad to hear that you're having fun. Did Gramma make you something to eat last night?"

Holding the phone tight against her ear, Tara sat down on the wooden bench. "Yep, she made supper and then we sat out on the porch while Big Joe worked in his garden. Gramma gave me a lemonade."

"Did you go to bed early like I told you to? Where did you sleep?"

Before coming to Gramma's, her mother had told her that she wasn't allowed to stay up late. But on Friday nights *The*

Dukes of Hazzard was on TV, so by the time she'd gone to bed it was almost midnight. She decided to answer the second question instead.

"I slept on the couch, but I wasn't scared," she said.

"Well, I think it's better if you sleep in Nana's old room, Tara, because you shouldn't be sleeping in that living room all by yourself."

Tara couldn't sleep in Nana's room. It was right beside the attic room and she would have a heart attack if she slept there all alone!

"They didn't tell me to sleep upstairs, Mommy. I don't want to sleep up there," she said.

"Tara, put Gramma on the phone," her mom said, raising her soft voice.

"Wait, Mommy, I wanted to ask you a question. Have you ever seen Joey's room?"

There was silence for a minute and then her mom said, "Well, of course I have…it used to be my room."

Tara hadn't realized it was her mom's old bedroom. It was hard to picture her mom having lived in Gramma's house before.

"I was in that room for two years before I left home," her mom explained. "It's not a nice room; it doesn't have a doorknob and the door doesn't even shut all the way. It's actually a yucky room—you shouldn't go in there."

"Did you know that the curtains are made of paper?" Tara asked. "They are blue and white."

"Oh my God, does she still have those ugly old curtains on the window? Poor Joey. You would think that, after all these years, she might have bought him some new ones." Tara heard her mom mumbling to herself. "I'm going to need to invite Joey here to Kitchener and have a nice long visit with him. See how he's doing. It's been too long since we've talked…"

"—Mommy? Do you know Walter Glass Whiskey?" Tara wanted to know more about the man across the street.

"What the heck? How do you know him?" Her mom's voice got louder, and she sounded a bit mad. After a moment, and with a sigh, she said, "Walter was a man who used to come around when I was little. I don't think he liked me, and I really didn't like him. Anyway, now he's just the man who lives across the street. Why he lives there I don't know, but he's not important and I don't know why Mom is telling you about him. Put her on the phone now, please."

"OK, Mommy. Gramma and I are going to go uptown this afternoon. She wants to show me off. And she's going to take me to the library to get me a book. And then we're going to the A&P and she said I could put a quarter in the dog's head."

"Well, that sounds nice, Tara, I hope you have fun." Her mom's voice sounded kind of flat now, so Tara thought she better just go and get Gramma.

"'Bye, Mommy. I love you."

"Oh, wait, Tara. I love you too, and I miss you already." Her mom's voice had softened again. "Don't worry about getting Gramma, I'll just say goodbye now."

"OK, 'bye again. I love you…again."

Tara could hear Gramma opening another can of cat food for Smokey as she called from the kitchen. "Does your mom want to talk to me now, dear?"

"No, Gramma, she had to go."

Tara stood on the wooden bench to hang the heavy phone back in its cradle, and then sat down again for a moment before going back into the kitchen.

Why did Mommy sound mad? She wondered. *Why didn't she want to talk to Gramma at the end?*

Maybe she wouldn't ask so many questions the next time her mom called.

"Time to get ready for our walk so get your shoes on, Lucy," Gramma sang as she came into the front hall holding up Tara's white leather sandals.

Tara loved when Gramma sang funny songs to her, or recited the many poems and nursery rhymes that she knew. She always had one ready and one of her favourites was *There Was a Little Girl, Who Had a Little Curl*. It went on to say that the girl with the curl was very, very good, but horrid when she was bad. Tara was happy to know that Gramma thought she was "very, very good".

"Gramma, is it going to be a long walk?" Tara asked as she slipped on her sandals. "Do you know how to get all the way uptown?"

"Well, sure I do. C'mon now!" Gramma opened the door and Tara went out, closely followed by Smokey. "Oh, no you don't, mister. You stay inside while we're out. I don't want you getting hit by a car."

Once Gramma had put Smokey back in the house, they set off down the sidewalk and up the embankment toward the train tracks.

"Will a train come and hit us, Gramma?" Tara looked nervously up and down the tracks.

"Not if we hurry up," Gramma said, teasing. "But, seriously, Tara, don't you ever cross these tracks by yourself. Do you hear me? You never know when a passenger train will come speeding by, and that will be the end of you. Toot toot, peanut butter!"

It was a hot summer day and the sun was shining brightly on their faces, but there was a nice breeze and Tara could feel it gently moving her thin brown hair out of her eyes. Once they'd passed all the old houses with their deep porches and large, leafy shade trees, they found themselves on the sunny streets of uptown Stratford.

"Where are we?" Tara asked, looking around. She felt like they had walked a long way, and wondered if they were lost.

"This is called Wellington Street, dear. Your mommy and I used to live right up there."

Gramma pointed to a couple of large windows above a stationary store.

"Is that Mrs. Wrenn's house?" asked Tara.

Gramma looked at her quickly out of the corner of her eye. "No. We lived on Wellington Street after we lived at Mrs. Wrenn's house. How do you know about her?"

"Mommy always talks about her," said Tara. "She says that Mrs. Wrenn was really mean."

"Well, I must say that I remember your mom talking about her when she was young, and I remember thinking at the time that maybe Cathy didn't like living by Mrs. Wrenn's rules. She didn't like having to help clean up after supper, and she didn't like running errands for Mrs. Wrenn when she needed something from the store. Mrs. Wrenn wasn't such a bad lady… she came to visit me up at the hospital last spring when I was in with pneumonia."

"Mommy said that Mrs. Wrenn visited her at the hospital too, one time," Tara said. "It was when she had Ronnie. Mommy said she was real mad that Mrs. Wrenn came into her room."

"I don't know why your mommy hated Mrs. Wrenn so much. I don't think she hardly even spent time with her. I mean it was only for a few minutes after school, and then I was home right after work to take care of my Cathy-O."

Tara felt confused because her mom and Gramma seemed to have different feelings about Mrs. Wrenn. Not really understanding, and starting to get hot, she asked, "Are we going to be at the library soon?"

Tara was relieved to enter the cool quiet of the library, where she and Gramma spent a long time choosing books for themselves. On the way back home they stopped by the liquor store and carried home a few bottles in brown paper bags. Tara noticed that one of the bottles had that light-brown stuff in it— like the bottle that Gramma kept behind Big Joe's couch.

"You can draw on these bags for a while when we get home, dear," said Gramma, "then Big Joe will take us up to the A&P to get the groceries. Is there anything special you want from the grocery store?"

"Maple walnut ice cream, Gramma, because I know it's your favourite!" Tara was already looking forward to settling down on her couch with a big bowl of ice cream to watch their favourite TV shows. She hoped *The Love Boat* would be on, or maybe *Fantasy Island*.

She took Gramma's hand in hers and looked right and left before they crossed the tracks. They made their way down the embankment and back into the quiet of the house.

CHAPTER FIVE

Summer 1979—Sunday at Gramma's House

Tara woke up to the sound of rain coming down hard against the front window.

She opened her eyes a crack to see if it was daylight yet, and time to get up, but she couldn't be sure because the room was so dim. She listened for the usual morning sounds. Gramma coughing and blowing her nose, and Big Joe grunting short answers to her questions. Tara heard a faint voice coming from the kitchen radio. The voice seemed to go on and on…there was no singing at all.

She crawled to the other end of the couch and peered around the doorway into the kitchen. Gramma was pouring some of the light-brown liquid from the bottle into her tea cup, and then she poured a bit into Big Joe's cup too.

"Morning, Gramma! Who's that talking on the radio?"

Gramma quickly put the cap back on the bottle and walked into the back part of the living room. She leaned over and put the bottle on the floor behind Big Joe's couch.

"C'mon now, dear. Come into the kitchen and we'll listen to the Sunday prayers. You can have Special K for breakfast and a piece of toast with honey on it. Then, once you're finished, we'll need to get crackin' for church. And make sure you grab your sweater because it's chilly today."

"Are you coming to church too, Big Joe?" Tara asked.

"No, I no go today. I have to look at garden," said Big Joe. "You go with Gramma. I take you."

Tara and Gramma dressed in their church clothes, grabbed an umbrella and their jackets, and got cozy in Big Joe's perfectly clean car. He turned the heat on high, checked the rearview mirror several times before backing out of the driveway, and then slowly and carefully drove through town toward St. Joseph's Catholic Church. Tara thought that Big Joe drove much slower than her mom did. Her mom was like a race-car driver!

"My Joe is a very good driver and he's taking his time on account of all this rain," Gramma explained, as if she could hear Tara's thoughts. After a few minutes of looking out the window, she added, "Good Lord, I hate the rain. It really gets on my nerves—it pains my back and gives me a godawful headache." She reached into her purse and pulled out several used tissues, her bank book, and a compact mirror, before she finally fished out her bottle of ASAs. She popped two of the pills into her mouth, not even needing a drink of water to swallow them down. "There, that should do the trick."

Big Joe pulled over to the side of the road, stopping just below the steep steps that led to the large front doors of the church. Tara held Gramma's hand as they slowly climbed up the stairs and then Gramma led her to the front of the church, where they found seats on the left-hand side. Tara took her sweater off and got settled into the pew, holding the hymn book in her lap. The church was filling up quickly as people came in out of the rain, shaking off their jackets and their umbrellas and getting themselves organized. The organist played the processional hymn while the ushers helped people find their seats and the nuns filed in from the side door and took their seats in the front pew.

Tara loved the hush of the church; the quiet murmuring of the congregation greeting each other over the smell of incense and burning candles. The church was much bigger, and more beautiful, than the one she and her mom went to in Kitchener. To Tara, it seemed like St. Joseph's was like a magical fairy place that she'd read about in her library books. She spent the next hour gazing at the beautiful stained-glass windows, the Stations of the Cross, and the altar with its fresh flowers and draping embroidered cloth. She loved being in this church with Gramma, although she did think the confession boxes lined up along the side were a bit creepy.

"Peace be with you, dear," Gramma said near the end of the service, taking Tara's hand and giving it a gentle squeeze.

"Peace be with you, too, Gramma," Tara said back, proud that she'd remembered the right words to say.

After Gramma had gone up to receive communion and the last hymn had been sung, they shuffled out of the church and down the steep steps to wait for Big Joe to pick them up again.

Once the three of them got back to 98 Railway Avenue, Big Joe said he was going to the Legion. Tara knew that was a place where people who'd fought in the war went to have a drink and play darts. Tara asked Gramma if they could watch cartoons, but Gramma said no, not on Sundays. Tara wondered what they would do instead.

"I'll put the kettle on and we'll have a hot tea to get rid of the damp, how does that sound?" asked Gramma.

Tara loved drinking tea. Everyone in her family did. Gramma liked hers steaming hot with Carnation milk, and Tara liked hers lukewarm with Carnation and lots of sugar. They took their cups into the living room and Gramma turned on all the lamps then started going through her record collection.

"Well, what do you say? Harry Hibbs or Nana Mouskouri?" asked Gramma as she flipped through the albums. "Bobby Vinton, maybe?"

"Harry Hibbs, please. I love "I'se da B'y"!" Tara put her cup down and started doing the Irish jig that Gramma had taught her the last time she visited.

Gramma laughed, tapped her toe, and lit a cigarette. "You know what, dear? I was tickled pink when your mom told me you were coming here for two whole weeks this summer. I hadn't seen you since the spring, and I was after missing you." Gramma took another sip of her cooling tea. "I'm not sure if you knew this, but I was really sick when you were here in May."

Tara remembered that awful May weekend clearly. Nana had still been living at Gramma's at the time, and Tara and her mom had planned to go to Stratford to visit her. Tara's mom said that Tara could stay the weekend to spend more time with both Gramma and Nana. They were all having a nice visit but then, just before her mom left, she and Gramma had gotten really mad at each other—or at least her mom had gotten mad at Gramma. Tara couldn't really understand what they'd been upset about, but it had had something to do with Nana and money.

After her mom left for Kitchener, Gramma had starting going around and around the house, blowing her nose and wiping her eyes with old tissues from her apron pocket. She'd been going up and down the basement stairs between doing laundry, washing and drying a mountain of dishes, and trying to get supper ready for everyone. She'd kept going to the cupboard to get more pills and then she'd started sweeping the floor.

"I have to get this house in order," she'd kept muttering. "It's important that I make sure you two are taken care of properly."

Tara and Nana had been sitting at the kitchen table playing cards, Nana watching Gramma out of the corner of her eye. When Gramma had put the dustbin in the fridge, Nana got up out of her chair, went straight to the phone and called Dr. Wilson. He'd arrived at the house in less than ten minutes. He'd checked Gramma over, and then he'd called a taxi to take her up to the Stratford General Hospital. Nana had called Tara's mom to ask her to come back to Stratford. A few hours later, after her mom had finished making supper for Nana and Tara, she'd spoken to the doctor on the phone. The doctor had told her mom that Gramma had the flu, bronchitis, and pneumonia—all at once!

Tara sat down on the couch when the record player switched songs to "Black Velvet Band" and picked up her cold teacup. "Are you feeling OK now, Gramma?"

"Oh yes, dear, I'm fit as a fiddle now. But I must say that I wish it would stop raining. The rain always makes me feel so lonesome, makes me feel so sad, but I don't know why. I guess it's just that, whenever it rains, I think about poor Daddy and how much I miss him. And I think about Cape Breton and how much I want to go back there to visit my family. And now it's making me miss Mama. Even though I know she's happy at Big Molly's, I wish she was still here with me. I hope she comes back to Ontario soon."

Tara felt a prickle behind her eyes and thought about how she missed Nana, too. She realized that maybe she also missed her mom, but she didn't want to think about her mom right now. Suddenly remembering all the fun toys hidden away in the wooden bench, she asked, "Can I get the bowling game out of the bench, Gramma?"

For the next hour, Tara played with the bowling ball and pins, coloured on the paper bags from the liquor store, and listened to Bobby Vinton's "Roses are Red" and "Blue Velvet." Gramma filed and polished her yellowed fingernails, and wrote in her diary. Once her polish was dry, she checked *The Beacon* to see what the Sunday TV matinee was.

"Oh, look! They're playing *A Nun's Story* at three o'clock. That's a good one," she said as she checked her watch. "Tara, go look in the buffet and bring over those photo albums that are in there. We can look at pictures while we wait for the movie to start."

Tara had seen these picture albums many times before. If there was one thing her family loved, it was looking at old photos.

"Let's start with the album with the purple flowers, Gramma, I love that one!" Tara helped clear the table beside Gramma's chair. She moved the ashtray, the pill bottles, the Kleenex box, the writing tablet, and Gramma's diary onto the floor. She then placed the album on the table and faced it toward Gramma.

"Now, let's see," Gramma said as she leaned over to get a better look at the first page. "Can you rhyme off all the names I taught you, dear?" She pointed to the famous family photo, taken when she was twenty-one years old, in Cape Breton. It was of her father and her mother and all her younger siblings. "You know that everyone's last name is Barron, but do you know their first names?"

Tara loved this name-guessing game. She almost never made a mistake. "There's Papa and Nana and you. Then Uncle Doug, Aunt Kay, and…Alice."

"Yes, that's right. My sister Alice. Do you like her red hair?"

Red hair? Tara thought. It was a black-and-white picture. She didn't see any red hair. Gramma always talked about her own wavy black hair and how silky and long it had been when she'd worn it in the pageboy style, which was popular when she was young. Her short hair was permed now, and it had started fading to grey here and there, but she said it suited her now that she was in her fifties.

"Is it OK to have red hair, Gramma?" Tara asked, still thinking about Alice's hair.

"Of course it is, dear." She pointed at the photo and continued. "Alice still lives on Cape Breton Island with her husband, Johnny, and their three. She'll never leave Cape Breton, that one, so you won't have to worry about meeting her anytime soon. Who's next?"

"Well, there's Big Molly, Tussie, Mickey…Francis. We don't like Francis, do we, Gramma?"

"Tara, who said that? My goodness! Don't you worry about him. Now go on."

"Then the youngest ones, Joanie and Rosie. Am I right?" Tara asked.

Gramma smiled. "You are a clever girl, Tara. How did you get so smart?"

They went through the rest of the photos, Tara guessing everyone's name correctly while Gramma told her what they were up to.

"Uncle Doug and his wife Elsie live in Stratford, pretty close to here, and I go to their place every couple weeks to help with the laundry and have a nice visit. You know, they never had children." She glanced up from the album and looked right at Tara. "Did you know that Elsie is as old as Mama?"

Tara hadn't known but realized that Aunt Elsie *did* look a little older than Uncle Doug.

"Now, where were we?" Gramma said, looking back at the pictures. She ran her polished fingernail across another photo. "Big Molly, God love her, is also in Cape Breton with her husband and their eleven children. Can you imagine? Ten girls and one boy. How on earth do you take care of ten girls?

Anyway, I love every last one of those children and they love me too." She continued, commenting on the next image. "Alright now, there's Tussie. Tussie lives in what they call the 'Row' with her two."

"What's the 'Row', Gramma?" Tara asked.

"Oh, well, I guess that sounds funny when I just say it like that, doesn't it?" Gramma laughed. "The 'Row' is just what we call the area of town where Row Street is. Tussie's lived in the 'Row' since years. Anyway"—her voice dropped to a whisper—"she and her husband separated many years ago."

She turned another page. "Ah, and there's my brother Mickey, we love him so much," she continued. "He's Mama's favourite, don't ya know? Well, he lives in Kamloops with his wife Alma and their five children. And there's Francis. He has a wife named Wilma and they live in Cape Breton. And that's all I have to say about him." Gramma paused then went on. "That's my sister Joanie. She's married to Stan Padacz. You know them. They live in Stratford, just down the street from here with their four children. I talk to Joanie every day. We are very close, her and I." She flipped another page. "Here's my youngest sister, Rose. She and her husband and their little girl—did you know that Rose's little girl is the same age as you?—all live about an hour from here, in Mount Forest." She pointed to the picture beside it. "And my sister Katie. You know her as Aunt Kay, and your mom took you to visit her before. Your mom really loves her Aunt Kay. They have a very special bond, they always have. Anyway, she lives in Brantford with her five children." She got quiet for a moment and then said, "Her husband Frank Larion died a few years ago now, God rest his soul." Gramma made the sign of the cross, as she always did when she mentioned anyone who had passed away. "Frank had a brother named Reg."

"Oh, I heard of Reg Larion. That's Mommy's daddy," Tara said, proud that she'd remembered her mom telling her about the Larions. "But we don't know him, right?"

"Yes, that's right." Gramma sat back and lit a cigarette. "It's all in the past now and I don't like talking about him, but I will tell you that I loved him—and that he didn't love me. Did you know that when we were dating he was already planning on marrying someone else?"

Tara knew he'd married someone else, but she was getting confused about who'd been dating who and when, so she mentioned what her mom had told her. "Mommy said that Reg was her daddy, but he didn't want her."

"Oh." Gramma fished a tissue out of her apron pocket and blew her nose. "Did she tell you that?"

"Yup. Mommy said that she was sad about it when she was little, but now she doesn't care anymore. But she always gets sad when she talks about him."

After a minute, Gramma said, "I feel awful that she's sad about Reg Larion. You know, she never asks me about him. We've never really talked about it, her and I. But I don't think it's that he didn't want to be her daddy. It was me he didn't want." She wiped her eyes and stubbed out her cigarette in the overflowing ashtray. "Well, dear, I think that's enough pictures for today. I think the show's coming on soon anyway."

—————————•∽∾•—————————

They watched *A Nun's Story* until Big Joe came home from the Legion looking for his supper. After a quick meal of cooked ham, boiled potatoes, and green peas, Tara felt gloomy all of a sudden and her throat felt a bit sore. She went and sat down on the couch and absently rubbed her chest. She hoped she wasn't getting a cold or something.

"Are you OK, dear? Does your chest hurt?" Gramma asked, looking concerned.

"Maybe a little bit. Do you think I'm getting one of your pneumonias?"

"Oh, no, not pneumonia, but maybe just the beginning of a cold. Here, let me get the Vicks. That will make you feel better in a jiff."

Gramma took a big dollop of Vicks vaporub and gently rubbed it onto Tara's thin chest. It felt warm and smelled funny, but at the same time, smelled like the kind of medicine that worked. After Gramma settled Tara's shirt back over her chest, Tara sank down into the cushions and thought of her mom.

The rain hadn't stopped all day, and it was turning into a dark and damp night. For a moment, Tara wished she could get into the flannel nighty she had at home and crawl into bed with her mom to watch TV on the old set she had in her bedroom.

"Gramma, can I call Mommy?" asked Tara.

Big Joe was resting on his couch after his big meal and said, from across the room, "No, you don't need call Mommy. Too late!"

Gramma glanced over at Big Joe but he had already turned over and started snoring again. "Well, it's a bit late, dear, but you can call her. You just have to be quiet while Joe's having his nap. Here, I'll dial the number for you."

"I know the number, Gramma. It's five-seven-eight, three-four-four-nine." Tara lifted the heavy telephone to her ear and pulled the metal dial around with her finger. She was relieved to hear her mom answer on the second ring.

"Hi, little girl! What are you doing calling me so late?"

Hearing her mother's soft voice made Tara's throat tighten up and her eyes prickle.

"Mommy, I miss you!" Tara started crying and she didn't know why. "Mommy, can you come and get me?"

Suddenly, Big Joe came flying in from the living room. "I said too late! You hang up right now." He took the phone from Tara's hands and hung it back up in its cradle. "You don't cry! No cry!"

"Now, Joe, she's just a little girl and it's late and she misses her mom." Gramma put her arm around Tara and pulled her close. "She's not used to you yelling. You're scaring her!"

Big Joe's wide blue eyes softened and the colour in his cheeks slowly drained away. "Oh," he mumbled as he rubbed his eyes. "I get you ice cream, OK? You watch TV with Smokey, I be right back." Big Joe limped off into the kitchen.

Leaning into Gramma, Tara did her best to stop crying. She didn't want to get in any more trouble.

"Don't worry, dear, I'll call your mom back and tell her that we hung up by mistake. You go get comfy on the sofa and Big

Joe will bring you a bowl of ice cream," Gramma said as she steered Tara toward the living room. "He is sorry, Tara. He's just tired and he's still not feeling well from his heart attack last winter."

Tara did what she was told. She got on the couch, pulled the blanket up over her shoulders, took a deep breath, and started to feel better.

"Here, you take." Big Joe handed her the bowl while Gramma called her mom back to try and explain what happened. "Tomorrow," Big Joe said, "I let you put pink curlers in my hair like you do, OK?"

Big Joe only had a few hairs that he combed in a swoop from one side of his head to the other, and whenever he would let her Tara would pull out Gramma's bag of pink foam curlers and roll them into Big Joe's hair. He would laugh, his cheeks would get all red, and he'd even pose for Gramma when she got the Polaroid out.

Very quickly Tara forgot about how Big Joe had yelled at her, and with Smokey curled up on the floor between all three of them, they tuned into their favourite Sunday night TV shows: *All in the Family* and *The Carol Burnett Show*.

CHAPTER SIX

Summer 1979—Gramma has a Dream

Tara woke up to warm sunbeams dancing across her sleepy face. She loved the warmth of the sun, and was glad that it finally felt like summer weather again.

"It's going to be a scorcher today, Tara," Gramma said from her chair across the room. "I was wondering if you were going to sleep the day away."

"Hi, Gramma. What are we going to do today?" Tara asked as she stretched her arms and rubbed her eyes.

It was a Monday morning, but because it was summer vacation Big Joe didn't have to go to his job at the cement factory and Joey didn't have to go to school. Gramma and Big Joe still woke up early—up with the birds, as Gramma would say—to have their breakfast and their tea and listen to the radio in the kitchen. Joey would still be sleeping until it was time for him to go to his summer job early in the afternoon.

During the week, Gramma babysat a bunch of kids. At one time, there'd been four or five of them, but now that summer was here she was only babysitting Gary, Terri-Lyn, and Junior. Tara was excited to see them today because she knew that on hot days, like the one Gramma promised it would be, the kids got to go for a swim in the above ground pool next door.

As if she knew what Tara was thinking, Gramma said, "John from next door said that the pool is open. Gary and Terri-Lyn are already there, and Junior will be here in about an hour or so."

Gary and Terri-Lyn were John's grandchildren, and if he had to go to work, the kids would come to Gramma's for the day. Junior was the boy who Gramma had been babysitting since he was a toddler, and Tara had played with him many times before.

After Tara had had her breakfast, and got dressed and ready for the day, Gramma asked her to go outside to find Big Joe in his garden while she waited for Junior to show up. Tara put on her sandals and went around the back of the house and found Big Joe bent over, weeding the vegetable beds and watering the tomatoes.

"Hi, Big Joe," she said quietly.

"Hi, you," he said, standing up and putting his hands on his hips. "Can you get cardboard baskets from basement and bring to me?"

Tara headed toward the front of the house, but Big Joe stopped her. "No, you go in basement door."

Tara looked at the back of the house but didn't see a basement door. She looked at Big Joe with her eyebrows raised.

"I show. Follow me."

He went to the side of the house, and set deep into the brick wall was a small wooden door. Big Joe pulled the rusty handle and the door creaked open. Even though he was short, he had to duck to make sure he didn't hit his head on the way in. Once they were in the basement, Tara had to blink it was so dark and dusty. The ceiling was low, and it smelled musty and damp. Tara wondered if this was a secret room. She had been in the basement (Gramma called it the cellar) many times to help Gramma with the laundry, but she'd never been to this side of the basement before and had no idea there'd been a door to the outside tucked away within the thick outer wall.

Along the far interior wall, under a tiny, dirty window, were piles of cardboard baskets. Tara recognized the baskets from when her mom would come home from the market with one full of fruits and vegetables. Tara then realized that beside the baskets were two wooden steps leading to a landing, and from there, more steps going up to another wooden door.

"What's up there, Big Joe?" Tara asked as she peered up the steps.

"What you mean? It's kitchen." He furrowed his brow. "Gramma up there."

Tara felt silly. Of course the steps led to the rest of the house. But it was hard for her to imagine that this damp, smelly basement had been under their feet the whole time. Tara didn't want to think about this room being down here while she was all cozy on her couch up there.

They gathered the baskets and made their way through the cobwebs and the dust and back out the door. Tara blinked again as her eyes struggled to adjust to the bright sunlight.

After a few minutes of helping Big Joe put tomatoes in the baskets, Tara heard Gary and Terri-Lyn laughing and splashing around in the pool.

"You go now and play with friends." Big Joe smiled at her and patted her on the head. "You good girl, Tara."

Tara was happy to have helped Big Joe, and she felt better knowing they were back to normal after last night.

By the time Tara went back into the house to get her bathing suit on, Gramma was already dressed and ready for the pool. She was wearing her hot-pink one-piece bathing suit with her short-shorts over top.

"Junior's in the living room, and Gary and Terri-Lyn are on their way over for a quick lunch before we head back over to John's for the afternoon. I've got your bathing suit and towel ready up in the bathroom, so run up and get changed and I'll have this lunch ready in two shakes of a lamb's tail."

Up in the bathroom, Tara could hear the commotion as the kids barged through the front door, saying hi to Junior and asking where she was.

"I'm coming!" She called out as she anxiously waited for the stupid toilet to flush. She then hurled herself down the stairs and ran into the kitchen. The kids were already seated around the table, their peanut butter and jam sandwiches on saucers in front of them.

"Gary, you know that that's my cup! I always have the red one," Terri-Lyn yelled at her older brother.

"Which one's mine then?" asked Gary, as if he didn't already know.

"Mine is yellow, Terri-Lyn's is red, and yours is blue," said Junior calmly. "And Tara's is the green one. She always has the green one."

Tara really liked Junior, she always had. He reminded her of a teddy bear. He was the same age as her, but he was big and soft and had kind brown eyes. Gramma loved Junior and his mother. Gramma often said that Donna was kind and helpful, and was always there when she needed a hand. Gary, on the other hand, reminded Tara of Alfalfa from *The Little Rascals*— he was always up to something, and his little sister Terri-Lynn often complained and screeched at Gary for teasing her.

"OK, you kids, off you go to John's. I'll clean up and be right over," said Gramma as she smiled at them and swept them out the front door.

"I'll wait for you, Gramma," said Tara.

Once the dishes were put in the sink and the colourful Tupperware cups were rinsed out, they too headed out the door and over to John's backyard.

After the excitement of the pool, and once the kids had gone back home to their parents, the bathing suits had been hung up to dry, and supper was done, Gramma suggested that she and Tara go for a nice evening walk up to the Handy.

The Handy was one of Tara's favourite places to go. It was the neighbourhood variety store, and there was a nice lady who worked there named Lois. She was always behind a long glass counter which was full of candy, and whenever Tara went in Lois would give her a small paper bag and let her pick out whatever she wanted. She usually got enough candy to fill up the whole bag!

When Tara and Gramma arrived back at the house, Gramma said they should take a break and sit on the porch and enjoy the evening for a while.

"You know, I had a beautiful dream last night," she began as she lit a cigarette. "I was dreaming about poor Daddy. You know he's been gone since twenty-one years? He was trying to tell me something, but before he got a chance Big Joe woke me up."

Gramma sounded so disappointed and sad that Tara stopped eating her candy for a minute to listen more intently.

"You know I love Mama, your Nana, but I will always have a special place in my heart for Daddy. He was so kind and he worked hard and he loved me. I know he loved all his children, but I was his first and he was so proud of me when I left home to go and work for the war effort in Brantford. But then I got pregnant. You know, I did my best when I had your mommy. I kept her with me even though the nuns told me I should give her up, but nothing or nobody could take my Cathy away from me—and I wouldn't sign any papers. I guess you realize now, Tara, that I wasn't married at the time, but I raised her on my own until she got married when she was seventeen years old." She paused. "Anyway, I hope Daddy was proud of me. It just breaks my heart that he's gone."

Gramma made the sign of the cross before she took another cigarette out of its pack and lit it. She was quiet for a while as she slowly smoked and gazed down the road.

"Well, that's enough of that, isn't it?" she said as she snuffed her cigarette out in the ashtray. "What I really wanted to say was that, after my dream, I decided that I'm going down home to Cape Breton next summer and I want you to come with me!"

"Oh, Gramma! Yes, I want to go with you. I want to see Nana," Tara said. "But how will we get there?"

"We'll take a big plane, naturally. You will love it! When you're way up in the air, and you look out the window, all the cars look like tiny ants. You can't even imagine! We'll ask your mom the next time we talk to her, OK?"

———————◆◁∞▷◆———————

Tara's two-week visit at Gramma's was fun and full of sunshine—she even had a good time on the rainy days! She played with the kids, swam in the pool, and made several more trips to the Handy. Most nights, she and Gramma sat outside on the porch while Gramma talked about her family and friends and all her memories. Gramma could talk and talk, and Tara loved listening to her.

At the end of the visit Tara was sad to say goodbye, but she was also excited to get back home to her mom and her brother and their pets and the comfort of her own bed. She was especially looking forward to crawling into her mom's bed, where they spent their Sunday mornings watching TV, to tell her all the stories from her time at Gramma's.

"So, tell me everything," her mom said as she pulled the blankets up over their laps while they snuggled in the bed. "What was the best part of the whole thing?"

"It was all so much fun, Mommy. We went to church, to the A&P, and to the library, and Gramma and I went to the Handy almost every day, and we watched our favourite TV shows and had soft-boiled eggs, and I did my dance routine for them and at the end they called out 'Bravo!' to me. They love it when I sing and dance for them!"

"Wow, that's a lot of stuff, little girl." Her mom shifted under the blankets. "So, why were you asking me about Walter Glass Whiskey, of all people?"

"He was sitting on his porch across the street from Gramma's. He was always waving and Gramma said she knew him a long time ago, but that's all she said."

"Well, that's true. And I knew him, too, when I was just a bit older than you. Mom dated him for a long time but they never got married."

"So Gramma never married Reg Larion and she never married Walter Glass Whiskey?" Tara asked.

"That's right." Her mom put her arm around Tara's shoulders. "Maybe you're too young to hear these stories."

"I like when you and Gramma tell me stories. Gramma likes to talk a lot, and I like listening to her."

"Well, I'll tell you more when you're older, but for now I'll say that I never had a dad who loved me. I know that Reg Larion was, or I guess I should say *is*, my father, but I don't know him."

"Maybe he wants to meet you, Mommy."

"He knows who I am, but he's never asked to see me. He's never tried to meet me. There was a time when my Uncle Frank, his brother, tried to get us together, but Reg cancelled at the last minute."

"Gramma said that your Uncle Frank died," Tara said, looking at her mom closely.

"Yes, he did, God love him." She crossed herself. "You know, they say he was a complicated man but he was always nice to me and I loved him. But enough of all that for now. I shouldn't even be telling you this stuff. You're still only five-and-a-half. Tell me more about Junior and the other kids."

Tara talked and talked about Gary and Terri-Lynn and Junior and the pool and all the fun they had running around from one backyard to the next. She talked about helping Big Joe in the garden and discovering the secret part of the basement, and how she hadn't been scared even though she didn't like the musty smell.

When she was done, her mom asked, "So what happened that night when you hung up the phone on me? The first Sunday night you were there?"

"You mean after Gramma put the Vicks on my chest?"

"That's not what I meant, and I didn't know she did that. Was your chest sore?"

"Gramma was worried that maybe I was getting a cold, so she rubbed Vicks on me and it worked! I didn't get a cold after all."

Her mom squinted at her. "Well, that's nice that she did that. She has never in her whole life put any Vicks on me."

Maybe I shouldn't have told her that, Tara thought.

"No," her mom continued. "I mean when you called me on the phone and suddenly hung up. Mom said it was an accident, but I heard Big Joe's voice in the background."

Tara squirmed around a bit, trying to think of something else to talk about. She didn't like the memory of Big Joe getting mad at her, but she couldn't think of what else to say so she told her mom the whole story.

Her mom was quiet for a bit, and then she said, "Did he hurt you, Tara? Did he hit you at all?"

"Oh no! Big Joe would never hurt me. He thinks I'm a good girl. He always leaves me cookies."

"Well, that may be, but you said you were scared," her mom said.

"Gramma said I was scared, but I wasn't ... I was just a little bit afraid."

"Honey, that's the same thing. What happened afterwards?"

"Big Joe gave me a bowl of my favourite ice cream and said I could ask Smokey to sit with me," Tara said.

"That's odd. When I was a kid, he never gave me a bowl of ice cream after he got mad at me. And Mom never stuck up for me when I was afraid, that's for sure." Her mom sat up and drew her knees to her chest. "That must be nice for you, eh?"

Feeling uncomfortable and thinking that maybe she made a mistake or something, Tara asked, "Should I be mad at Big Joe, Mommy?"

Her mom reached over to the Kleenex box and wiped her eyes with a tissue. "Oh my goodness, Tara, no. You didn't do anything wrong, and you shouldn't be mad at Big Joe. I'm glad he loves you, and I'm glad Mom stuck up for you." Her mom put her arms around Tara and pulled her close. "Don't you worry—you're a good girl. Sometimes I get sad, so just ignore me," she said with a sigh.

"You always stick up for me, right, Mommy?" Tara didn't want her mom to be sad. "Remember that babysitter I had last year?"

"Oh, that mean old lady," her mom said. "How could I forget?"

Tara had only gone to the old lady's house for lunch, and then for a few hours in the afternoon until her mom came to pick her up after work. The woman was older—a grandmother—and her granddaughter had been there in the afternoons as well.

After lunch, the girls had to play in the backyard because the old lady didn't like them to be inside when it was warm and sunny outside. The backyard didn't have much to offer as far as anything to play with, but there was a pretty stone birdbath that stood in the middle of the yard, filled with clean, cold water. The granddaughter had asked for a glass of ginger ale and thought it would be funny to pour it into the birdbath. What would the birds think, the girls had wondered, when, instead of fresh, cold water, the birds got a taste of fizzy ginger ale? As soon as the granddaughter had poured the ginger ale into the birdbath, the old lady had swung open the screen door and screamed for the girls to get inside the house.

Tara remembered that the granddaughter had gone straight to the den to watch TV, not concerned about getting into trouble. Tara had wanted to follow the girl, but the old lady told her to sit in the front room and wait on the plastic-covered couch until her mom came. When her mother had arrived to pick her up, the old lady told her that Tara had been a very bad girl and had fed the poor birds ginger ale. Tara had tried to explain that it had been the granddaughter's idea, that *she* was the one who had poured the pop into the birdbath, but the old lady continued to blame Tara. Once Tara and her mom had gotten in the car to head home, Tara had tried again to explain that she wasn't to blame, that she wasn't a bad girl.

"Tara, don't you worry about that old lady," her mother had said. "I saw right through her, and I knew that she was just a miserable old thing. You will not be going back to her place again, that's for sure."

Tara remembered feeling relieved that she hadn't gotten in trouble, but at the same time she had been curious that her mom had such a strong reaction to the old lady. In fact, there were many times that Tara could recall her mother sticking up for her—whether it was because of a mean babysitter, or a teacher who hadn't treated her nicely.

"There are lots of people who are not very nice, little girl," her mom said, pulling Tara away from her memories of the old lady, "and I took you away from all of them as soon as I found out, didn't I? I would never let anyone be mean to you. Remember last fall, when your teacher called you Terrible Tara? Remember how I stuck up for you then?"

It was a day Tara couldn't forget. Tara liked to talk, and sometimes she talked too much during school. One day her kindergarten teacher, Mrs. Finlayson, had yelled at her to keep quiet in front of the whole class. Not used to getting in trouble, Tara's face had gone red and she'd fought hard to keep from crying. One of her best friends, a boy named Ewan, whispered that Mrs. Finlayson was terrible.

When the teacher heard the word, she'd said loudly, "Yes, that's right, Tara *is* terrible. She's *Terrible Tara*."

It took everything Tara had to keep her tears from falling during class, but as soon as she had gone home and told her mom what had happened she couldn't fight the tears back any longer. Her mom had taken one look at her daughter, grabbed her hand, and marched right back to the school. She'd found the classroom and stormed right up to Mrs. Finlayson.

"Don't you *ever* talk to my daughter like that again," she'd said through clenched teeth, "or I swear to God I will come back here and you will be sorry!"

Tara couldn't believe how mad her mom had gotten at Mrs. Finlayson, but secretly she was beaming with pride because she'd known that her mother would do anything and everything to protect her...even scare a teacher!

"My mother never would have done that," her mom said, pulling Tara closer. "She never stuck up for me, but I will always stick up for you, little girl. I'll never let anyone be mean to you."

Pulling the blankets up over their shoulders and snuggling down into the pillows, her mom turned on the little TV and said, "Let's see what those silly people are doing on *Coronation Street*."

CHAPTER SEVEN

Summer 1980—A Few Days in Stratford

Tara couldn't believe a whole year had gone by since she'd last spent time at Gramma's house by herself.

Every year, either Gramma, Big Joe, and Joey would try to come to Kitchener for Thanksgiving, Christmas, or Easter, or Tara's family would try to get to Stratford. But this past year neither family had travelled for these celebrations.

Tara kept asking her mom why they didn't go to see Gramma, but she never got a straight answer. Joey had once come to Kitchener for the weekend, and it had been nice, but Tara thought it was strange how he acted so differently at their house. He was happy and laughed and was easy to get along with. Tara didn't understand why he didn't act like that when he was home, at Gramma's.

Even though Tara hadn't gotten to see Gramma much throughout the year, she'd talked to her a lot on the phone. During the winter, Gramma had called to tell Tara that Nana's brother and sister had both died. Gramma had been upset... she'd loved her aunt and uncle and she knew how sad Nana would be, losing them so close together.

Gramma had called again in the spring with even more sad news. One day, Smokey had been hit by a car and died right in her arms. When Tara heard that, tears streamed down her cheeks. She'd loved that old cat, and she was going to miss him. She hoped he was catching mice up in Heaven.

But the good news was that Gramma and Big Joe had gotten a new cat, one with orange fur—so of course Gramma had named him Ginger. Tara was looking forward to meeting Ginger and hoped she'd be able to hold him in her lap.

The most exciting news, though, was that Gramma had asked her mom if Tara could go to Cape Breton with her for two weeks in July and her mom had said yes! Tara was beside herself. She'd never been on a plane before, she'd never left the province of Ontario before, and she'd never met the hundreds of cousins "down home" who Gramma had told her about. Gramma and her mom had always referred to Cape Breton as "down home," and Tara thought it sounded like a place she wanted to see.

———•⤙∞⤚•———

Tara was all packed up for the big trip to Cape Breton, but first her mom was taking her to Stratford to meet Ginger and relax for a few days before Big Joe would drive her and Gramma to the airport in Toronto. Tara was glad because she loved her summertime visits at Gramma's and hadn't wanted to miss it.

"Well, little girl, I can't believe you're going down home," her mom said as they got settled in the car for their drive through the country and on to Stratford. "When I was your age, all I wanted to do was go to Cape Breton and be with Nana and Janey and everyone else down there. You are a very lucky girl, and I think you're going to have a lot of fun."

Tara thought her mom sounded disappointed. *Maybe she wants to go, too?*

"Why don't you and Aunt Marlene come with us, Mom? Wouldn't you both like to see Nana?"

Tara's Aunt Marlene had come up to Ontario from Nova Scotia when she was just a teenager. Marlene had already been married to her husband Wendell, but she hadn't wanted to stay in Cape Breton so she and Uncle Wendell had gotten a place near Tara's parents. Soon after Tara was born, they'd had their son Shawn. Tara and Shawn were very close, and their families had done stuff together almost every weekend.

"We sure would, honey, but we both have to work and take care of our pets, and it costs a lot of money to buy plane tickets; we can't really afford it. But don't you worry about that. You just have a good time, and make sure you give Big Molly a hug and a kiss for me. You wouldn't remember this, but she came up to Ontario around the time you were born. She'd been here anyway because Janey and her husband had decided to move here, and during the only year they stayed, Janey had a set of twins. They were born a month before you, but Big Molly stayed for months after to help Janey with the babies."

Whenever her mom would tell Tara about the family members—their names, and where they lived—her head would start spinning. It was so confusing, keeping it all straight.

"I sure hope I can remember everyone's name once I get to Cape Breton," Tara said out loud, looking out the window.

Her mom smiled, turned up the radio, and rolled down the windows. Once again, Tara was excited to watch the horses and the cows and the farms and the barns go by at lightning speed.

After a little while, Tara asked, "Mom, can you sing that song I love?"

"That old Dickey Lee song? You don't want to hear that heartbreaking song again, do you?"

Tara's mom loved to sing more than she loved a lot of things, so she turned the music down and quietly began singing "Patches." Tara thought it was the saddest song she'd ever heard. It was about a boy and a girl who loved each other, but the girl, Patches, didn't think she was good enough for him so she drowned herself in that dirty old river.

"Oh, Mom, could you ever imagine doing that?" Tara asked.

"Well, I *did* almost do that. I was about thirteen or fourteen years old, and I was feeling so down. I wasn't happy, and I felt ugly and stupid and I didn't think anyone loved me. I was feeling this way for a long time, but nothing made me happy so I decided that I might as well drown myself."

Tara went completely still. *Is she joking?*

"I planned it all out," her mom continued. "I was going to go uptown and over to the Avon River. I was going to walk right in until the water went over my head and I couldn't breathe anymore."

"Mom! Are you kidding? Why would you do that?" Tara couldn't believe what she was hearing.

"Because, I told you, I was very sad. Anyway, there I was all ready to walk into the river, but when I went down the hill toward the bank I couldn't believe my eyes. The Avon River was dry! They'd drained the water and all that was left was mud, puddles of river water, and swan feathers. For God's sake, I thought, I couldn't even drown myself properly!" she laughed as she turned the car down Railway Avenue.

Many people in Tara's family laughed when they told a wild story like the one her mom just told her. They would tell an awful story and then say something like, "Well if you can't cry, you have to laugh."

As if what her mom described about drowning herself in the Avon River wasn't meant to be serious, she quickly changed the subject and said, "Oh, here we are at Mom's already."

Tara wasn't sure if her mom's story was true or if she was exaggerating, so she quickly forgot about it and jumped out of the car.

Gramma called out, holding open the screen door. "There's my doll! I'm glad you're here nice and early."

Tara ran to the porch and hugged her grandmother.

Her mom made her way up the steps with Tara's suitcase, firing off instructions to Gramma as she went. "OK, Mom. So I've packed Tara's health information if anything happens, and here's a list of phone numbers in case you forget your address book. I've packed everything that she should need although I didn't include any towels, but you're not taking her swimming in that ocean or anything so just having her bathing suit to play on the beach should be good enough. Is there anything else you need?"

"Do you want to come in so we can talk about all of this over a cup of tea, hun?" Gramma asked, gesturing her inside.

"Mom, I have to go. I don't have time for a visit. I already told you that on the phone."

"Well, Cathy, I don't think you need to worry so much. If we need anything we can always go into Glace Bay and get it. They still have lots of stores down there," Gramma said.

"Call me as soon as you land. Bring lots of change so you can make the long distance call on the pay phone. I'm going to worry, Mom, so please be sure to call me right away, OK?"

"Hun, don't you worry about a thing. Tara and I are going to be just fine," Gramma said, smiling at Tara.

Tara's mom took her hand and led her down the steps to the walkway. "Little girl, I want you to have a good time, but please be careful and do not go swimming in that ocean! It will carry you away and I'll never see you again."

Tara gave her mom a big hug and told her she'd be careful and wouldn't go swimming. Tara had taken swimming lessons at the local pool in Kitchener, but she figured the Atlantic Ocean and its waves were a lot different from the shallow end at the community pool.

After her mom took off down the road, honking as she went, Tara ran back up the steps and through the door.

Gramma gently closed the door and followed her inside.

"Alright, Gramma, where's that new kitten of yours? I'm dying to meet him!" Tara said, looking around.

"Oh, well, Ginger's not a kitten anymore, dear. He's almost eight months old now, but is he ever cute. C'mon, I've got him in the living room because I didn't want him getting outside."

While Tara played with Ginger, she and Gramma talked for a long time and got caught up, then they discussed their trip. They would be staying at Big Molly's house, and while she was there Tara would have a cousin to play with. At first Tara was surprised when Gramma had told her her cousin's name.

"Her name's Molly Ann, and she's Big Molly's granddaughter."

"Really? OK. So, who's Molly Ann's mom?" Tara asked. She was normally very good at remembering everyone's name, but this one was new to her.

"Her mom's name is Little Molly," Gramma said, answering with a grin.

"So wait, there's Big Molly, Little Molly, and Molly Ann?" Tara wondered if Gramma was teasing her.

"Yes, and there's Big Rita and Little Rita and Rita Rose. And Big Ralph and Little Ralph and Ralphina, and Big Alice and Little Alice and Big Kay and Little Kay…it just goes on and on like that."

"Gramma, are you being silly?" Tara couldn't believe it. "Why do they all have the same names?"

"That's just how it is, dear. But do you want to know something?

"Yes, what?"

"There's only one Tara, and that's you." Gramma leaned over and gave her a big hug.

That night, after supper was finished and the dishes were put away, and after Joey had gone out and Big Joe went to bed early, Tara and Gramma and Ginger settled in the living room to watch TV.

"Let's watch that new show, Gramma. It's called *The Incredible Hulk*."

"Oh, I think that's too scary for you, dear."

"No it's not. I think I've seen it before, and I wasn't scared," said Tara.

"Well, OK," Gramma said, relenting. "What channel is it on?"

At first everything was fine. Dr. Banner was a nice man who wasn't scary at all, then, all of a sudden he got angry. He'd said that no one would like it if he got angry. There were horrible sounds, sounds Tara had never heard before, and then Dr. Banner's skin started turning green and his clothes ripped and then his eyes turned green too.

Tara screamed and pulled the blanket over her head. "Turn it off, Gramma! I don't like those sounds!"

"It's OK, it's OK, the awful sounds have stopped," Gramma said. "He's just a big green guy now."

Tara peered out from under the blanket. Although the Hulk was big and angry, it wasn't as bad as when he'd been turning *into* the Hulk.

"Next time, Gramma, you'll have to turn the volume down so I can't hear that sound, and I'll hide until he turns into the Hulk, and then you tell me when it's safe to come out, OK?"

"I told you this was too scary for you," Gramma said, laughing. "Next time, we'll watch *The Dukes of Hazzard*."

———————◄◆◇►•———————

When Tara woke up on Saturday morning, she could hear the rain pounding against the windows. When she looked outside, everything was wet. Tara knew that with this rain she'd be staying inside all day, and wouldn't be able to see Gary and Terri-Lynn.

Gramma would complain about her aching head and her sore back and how the rain made her feel sad. Tara didn't like to see Gramma take pills all the time, but once Gramma had them along with her tea with the light-brown stuff in it, she would be happier and so maybe it was OK.

Tara had breakfast with Gramma and Big Joe, and all three of them watched Ginger play with a string Tara had found in the cupboard.

"Do you want to see the new dance I learned?" Tara asked her grandparents. She knew how much they loved when she put on her shows in front of the pantry.

When she'd finished showing them her latest routine, they applauded and Gramma asked for another.

"Wait," Big Joe said with a smile. "You teach me that! You teach me dance."

Tara laughed. "Big Joe, you can't dance!"

"Yes, you show me. I can do." He got up from the chair and made his way to the centre of the kitchen.

"OK, Big Joe, take my hand. Ready?" asked Tara. "This move's called hitchy-koo ball change."

"Heavens to Betsy, Joe!" Gramma laughed. "You'll break a hip, for God's sake!"

"Step together step, ball change. Step together step, ball change," Tara said, instructing her grandfather. "That's it!"

Big Joe's cheeks were bright red, and his eyes shone a bright blue. He said, "I show you something now."

He took both Tara's hands and began waltzing her around the room.

"Oh, would you look at that. How cute!" Gramma ran to get her Polaroid, but by the time she got back Big Joe needed a break and he had led Tara back to the kitchen table.

After a few minutes, Joey came into the kitchen from upstairs. He grunted a good morning to everyone then made himself some toast to take with him as he took off out the front door. Tara was surprised he hadn't headed into the living room to watch TV. *Maybe he's late for work because he's always sleeping in.*

Big Joe went to lie down on the couch, and Gramma and Tara sat quietly at the kitchen table.

"Can I get the photo albums out, Gramma?" asked Tara as she headed toward the buffet in the front hall where they were kept.

"Of course. Bring them in here and put them on the table," Gramma answered.

"Gramma, I haven't seen these ones before," Tara said, settling into her chair and opening to the middle of the album. "Which Christmas was this?"

"Oh, that's before you were even born, dear. I think it was 1972. Let me check the back. Yep, 1972." Gramma flipped the page. "Aww, would you look at Smokey. God love him." She crossed herself. "I really miss that old cat."

"I miss him too, Gramma." But Tara didn't want to think about Smokey. She'd loved him so much and didn't want to start crying, so she changed the subject. "Is this your tree?"

Tara looked closely at the Christmas tree in the picture. It was so different from their tree at home. This one didn't look real, and it was covered in silver garland and had colourful lights and lots of tinsel. Tara's mom only liked real trees with white lights, and she hated tinsel and garland. "It's all so fake," her mom would say.

In one picture, there were only a few gifts under the tree and they didn't look like they were wrapped very well. At home, the gifts were piled high and her mom always made sure the presents were perfectly wrapped, with matching ribbons and bows. Her mom always said that she didn't buy much during the year so she could spend all of her money on Christmas and all the things she could do to make it special. Tara and Ronnie looked forward to Christmas every year. It was a magical time, and their mom always made sure they had music and candlelight, food and drinks, decorations and a big homemade dinner. Their family get-togethers were always warm and welcoming.

Tara flipped the page and found a picture of Joey. In this photograph, he was a little boy and he was sitting all by himself under the sad-looking Christmas tree. He didn't look happy at all. Maybe he was lonely because even though Tara's mom was his half sister, Joey had been raised as an only child. Poor Joey. What would it be like to be the only child at Christmas?

Tara turned the pages backward until she found pictures of Joey as a toddler and then as a baby. There he was sitting on a blanket by the side of the house and playing with a ball, and there he was holding hands with Big Joe beside their car, and another one playing with their dog Pal, and a really cute one of him and Gramma in the kitchen with their bathing suits on. He looked happy in all these pictures, but when Tara turned to pictures of him at around twelve or thirteen years old, she was curious to see his eyes looked empty and sad.

Tara didn't know why Joey looked so sad in those pictures, but suddenly she thought his sad eyes looked like her mom's sad eyes in pictures from when she was a little girl. Tara felt bad and decided that maybe she wouldn't get so mad at Joey the next time he turned off her cartoons. Tara felt a pit growing in her stomach when she realized that maybe, when she was at Gramma's, she got more attention than Joey did. She wondered if maybe he didn't like how Gramma and Big Joe spoiled her so much when she was visiting. Tara started to feel a little sorry for Joey, and she realized then that she really did love her uncle. She decided that when she came back from Cape Breton she would try to be nicer to him so that his eyes didn't look so sad.

CHAPTER EIGHT

Summer 1980—Finally in Cape Breton

Tara couldn't get over it. Gramma had been right. The cars driving on the roads far below did look like tiny ants!

The plane was getting ready to land at the Sydney airport, but before it hit the runway it swooped out over the water, tilted to the side (Tara thought they were going to land in the ocean!), and then dropped from mid-air. Tara's stomach dropped too as she grabbed Gramma's bony hand.

"Hold on now, dear. We're just about there," Gramma said, laughing and leaning over to look out the window from her aisle seat.

Once they'd landed and gathered their suitcases, they found Big Molly's son Little Ralph waiting for them in his blue van to take them to Big Molly's.

The modest one-story house sat on a small piece of land just off Seaside Drive, the main road that wound its way up from the ocean and around Lingan Bay. The well-taken care of home had a little front yard and a larger backyard that led to the overgrown blueberry fields beyond.

When Tara and Gramma arrived, Tara couldn't stop staring at all the cousins. There were baby cousins crawling on the floor, kid cousins sitting on the furniture watching TV, adult cousins at the table drinking tea, and teenage cousins everywhere else. There were so many teenagers! Tara soon realized that they were all Big Molly's daughters.

She felt it would take a whole week just to learn their names, but then she remembered they all had the same names as their aunts. So all Tara had to do was figure out which one was which. But it still felt impossible!

"So, this is Tara! My God, I haven't seen you since years… you've grown into a big girl now, haven't ya?" Big Molly said as she took Tara's suitcase and brought it into one of the three bedrooms that were down the short hallway just off the kitchen.

The house was small but it had a large, open living room, a kitchen with lots of counter space, one tiny bathroom, and three medium-sized bedrooms: one for Big Molly, one for Nana, and one for all the girls who still lived at home. Little Ralph slept in another bedroom that was in the unfinished basement.

Tara looked all around, and finally spotted Nana sitting in the rocking chair in the corner of the living room. "Nana!" She ran over and wrapped her arms around her great-grandmother's neck. "I've missed you!"

"Hello, my dear. Lord, you're growing like a weed," she said as she continued rocking. "How's your mother, Cathy? Tell her I miss her. Can you ask her if she got my letter? Can you ask her to write me back?"

"I will, Nana. As soon as I get home, OK?"

"That's good, thank you. You run along now, dear. Go to the kitchen and get yourself something to eat," Nana said.

Back in the kitchen, the table was full of more relatives sitting around the table and eating cookies someone had brought to share.

"Hiya, Tara. Welcome home! My name's Molly, but everyone calls me Little Molly on account of my ma's name being Big Molly. She's not that big, really. She's actually pretty short, but anyway this here's my daughter Molly Ann. She's been beside herself all day waiting for you to get here, so you better both run along now and go outside and get some fresh air. Here, take these cookies with ya. They're prit' near all gone."

Tara didn't think Little Molly had taken a breath once while she was talking. Everyone here talked so fast, and they all had a thick Cape Breton accent. She realized that Gramma didn't have much of an accent at all. She'd have to ask her why the next time they got a chance to talk, because Molly Ann grabbed her hand and pulled her to the back of the house and out the screen door.

At the bottom of the stairs, parked in the long grass, was a tent trailer all set up and ready to go.

"We can sleep in there if you like," Molly Ann said as she opened the tiny door to show Tara the inside. "I'm so happy you're here. We're going to have lots of fun. We're going to pick blueberries, walk downtown, go to the beach, play with our cousins, and stay in the trailer every night. C'mon, let's go! I'll show you the blueberry patch!"

Molly Ann talked as fast as her mother and Tara had to listen carefully to correctly hear the words through her accent.

For a moment, Tara wondered where Gramma had gone off to, but before she could run back in the house to tell her that they were going to pick blueberries, Molly Ann had again grabbed her hand and began pulling her out of the backyard and through the fields.

————•◁∞▷•————

Tara spent the next two weeks playing with all her new cousins, getting to know her great-aunts—Tussie and Big Molly—and Little Molly and all of her younger, teenaged sisters. The girls' room had three sets of bunk beds and the sisters would invite Tara to come in and hang out with them. To Tara, it felt a lot like one of the senior girls' cabins at the summer camp she went to every year.

The sisters showed her their makeup, let her dress up in their clothes, let her read their teen magazines, and told her stories of their friends at school and the dances they went to on the weekends hoping to meet cute boys. The sisters were a lot older than Tara but they were very nice, and Tara felt comfortable being around them. By the end of the two weeks, she'd memorized all their names and who they'd been named after.

One sunny morning, Tara and Molly Ann woke up in the warm tent trailer and were surprised to hear all kinds of commotion coming from the house. They ran inside to see what was going on.

"We're going to the beach, girls," said a dark-haired woman who looked to be in her midtwenties. Tara hadn't met this cousin before, but she soon found out her name was Fina, short for Ralphina. "Get your shoes on, Tara, and get in the van!"

The big blue van was already crowded with cousins, coolers, picnic baskets, blankets, and towels.

Molly Ann climbed in behind Tara and grinned like a hyena. "Wait till you see where we're going, Tara. It's called The Cubby, and we have to hike all the way down the cliff to the beach below. We can spend the whole day there, but when the tide starts to come in we have to hurry and get back up the cliff before the ocean takes us all the way to Ireland."

Tara thought about her mom, and how upset she would be if she knew Tara was going to The Cubby with the chance she might be swept away. She'd make sure not to tell her mom this story when she got home.

Fina was one of Big Molly's older daughters, and she and her husband and their three lived over on Wallace's Road near the cemetery. She was a no-nonsense person, kept everyone in line, and didn't take any sauciness from anyone. But she had a kind heart, and kept an eye on every child like a hawk.

"No kid's gonna drown out here on my account," she said as she stood on the shore with her legs wide apart and her arms crossed over her chest. She stood for hours squinting at every child in the rough, wavy water.

After they got home from the beach and had changed into dry clothes, Molly Ann suggested they go downtown and buy some ice cream.

"Are we allowed to go by ourselves?" Tara asked. "We're only six years old, after all."

"Yeah, but we're prit' near seven, so we can go. Besides, everyone up and down the street knows who we belong to, so we'll be fine. C'mon!"

There was something about walking down to the store in Cape Breton that really affected Tara. It wasn't just the warm sunshine, the salty ocean breeze, and the constant sound of seagulls searching for old french fries. It was more about the weeds growing through the cracks in the pavement, that none of the houses had fences or fancy lawn furniture, and that when people sat outside they didn't sit in their backyards hidden away from passersby but were on their front porches, right up against the sidewalk happy to chat with anyone who walked by. No one was a stranger. Everyone was someone you knew. Life in Cape Breton was laid back, relaxing, and welcoming.

It felt good to be free and independent, and to not have to tell everyone where you were going all the time, knowing that everywhere you went someone knew your family. And if they didn't know you specifically, they assumed you belonged to someone they knew.

Tara remembered when Little Molly had said, "Welcome Home." It was a simple thing to say, but for some reason it now made Tara's throat tighten up. *Why would they welcome me home if I've never been here before?*

It was because, she realized, she belonged to someone they loved. She understood, now, that if someone from Cape Breton loved you, even if you lived all the way up in Ontario, then other Cape Bretoners naturally loved you too. And you could feel it. Tara had felt it when she'd realized that the front door of Big Molly's house was never locked.

One evening she'd asked if someone was going to lock the door before they went to bed and they all looked at her, real curious.

"What for?" they'd asked. "If we lock the door, how will the neighbours get in to get a hot cup of tea? How will they get in early in the morning for their toast before work? How will all our family get in and out whenever they need to if the door's locked?"

Tara remembered one particular morning, around when she'd first arrived at Big Molly's. She'd woken up early and thought she'd be the first one in the kitchen to put the kettle on for everyone, but when she stepped into the kitchen a man was already sitting at the table having his tea.

"Mornin' to ya," he'd said as he gestured for her to sit. "Up early, eh? Before the birds!"

"Yes, I am," Tara had said, moving slowly toward the offered chair. "Are you one of my cousins?"

"Lord, no! I'm Johnny from down the street. I just dropped by for a hot cup and a bit of toast before I head off to work."

And that's how it was. Big Molly's house was like a revolving door; you never knew who was coming or going. It was chaotic to Tara, but soon she began to anticipate the days and looked forward to the fun-loving craziness of the house. Instead of confusing, it became comforting. Everyone who passed through that door cared about you, and wanted to know who you were.

Tara loved early evenings, when Big Molly would put a roast in the oven, boil a humongous pot of potatoes, and bake her own homemade bread. Nothing could beat the smell of baked bread, and Big Molly was famous for it. Tara was allowed to set the table and every evening, she'd ask, "How many should I set it for, Big Molly?"

If there were ten expected, Big Molly would tell her to set it for eleven.

"I don't understand, why do you want it set for eleven if there's only going to be ten of us?"

"Well, dear, God always wants us to set an extra place, so if anyone unexpected comes, they will always feel welcome."

For some reason that made Tara want to cry. Each night she would sit at the table and stare at that spot and think about how whoever came to sit there would be sent by God. She figured the spot would remain empty, but almost every time someone came in from up the road they were thankful for the warm kitchen, the freshly baked bread, and the friendly company.

No wonder Tara's mom always talked about Cape Breton, and how much she missed it. Tara realized that it wasn't just the family she missed, it must have been the feeling of acceptance and love that emanated from the house itself.

Tara and Molly Ann bought their ice cream and walked the rest of the way down the road to the beach. They fed the remains of the cones to the screaming seagulls, and spent a few hours collecting shells and sea glass until they figured it was time to go back to Big Molly's for supper.

A few days after they'd arrived in Cape Breton, Gramma had been invited to Ingonish to visit with her cousins, Marie and Marjorie Barron. Gramma said that some of her best childhood memories where from when her daddy would take the family to Ingonish for long visits in the summertime. Tara was invited to go along, too, but she said she'd rather stay with Molly Ann and she'd see Gramma when she got back.

One afternoon, Tara came in from playing outside with Molly Ann and found Gramma sitting at Big Molly's kitchen table having some toast and tea.

"Gramma!" She gave her a big hug. "Did you have fun in the Ingonish place you went to?"

"Oh, Tara! It was wonderful! I haven't seen my cousins since thirty-four years, and it felt so good! We laughed and laughed, but I must tell you I cried my eyes out when I had to leave. We had a grand time, but being in Ingonish really made me miss Daddy. I kept thinking I'd see him coming up the road, but when I looked he was never there. Then I realized that poor Daddy is dead and gone to Heaven, and my heart broke all over again." Gramma crossed herself as she always did when she spoke of the dead, lit a cigarette, and took another sip of tea.

Tara felt sorry for Gramma. Whenever she talked about her father she got real upset. Tara knew that her mom had loved him—her Papa—too. Her mom said that her Papa had always been very kind to her, and that she'd only been seven years old when he was hit by a train and died. Tara wished that she could have met Papa, who she understood to be her great-grandfather, so she could see what he was really like.

Quickly wiping her eyes with a tissue and putting it away in her pocket, Gramma said, "I'll tell you more about Ingonish later, dear, but for now I'm going to finish this toast and then get ready to go to my sister, Tussie's. She's having me for supper. Are you alright to stay here with Mama and Big Molly if I go over there?"

"I don't mind at all if you go to Tussie's, Gramma."

To be honest, Tara liked being by herself in the house with all the cousins and she was looking forward to tonight because her mom's closest cousin Janey was coming over. It was true, that technically Janey was her mom's cousin but they acted more like sisters. Her mom and Janey acted like sisters with Aunt Marlene, too. Her mom often said they were like three peas in a pod.

Gramma left Tara her last bite of toast and marmalade, and a sip of her tea, and off she went in a taxi to Tussie's place down in the "Row".

That night, after the supper dishes were washed and put away and the table was wiped clean, Tara decided to play Solitaire at the kitchen table while Big Molly, Nana, and Janey sat in the living room. The house was strangely quiet because there was a big dance going on in Glace Bay and all the cousins had gone leaving Tara behind. Tara looked forward to the day that she could go to the dance, too—it sounded like so much fun. But for now she busied herself by playing cards and listening to the women talk in the other room.

"When do you think Cathy will write me back, Big Molly?" It was Nana who'd asked and Tara could hear her rocking chair creaking back and forth.

"Mama, you only just sent the letter last week. It's going to take her a few days to reply," Big Molly answered.

For a moment, Tara stopped playing cards and strained to hear what the women were saying. *Why does Nana keep going on about writing letters to Mom?*

"Well, ever since Rita told me that she wanted to take me back to Ontario, I've been worrying," Nana said.

Tara knew that Nana had lived with Gramma in Stratford for a few years, in the past, but wasn't exactly sure why. She knew Nana once had her own house here in Cape Breton, at 9 Woodward Street, when her husband had been alive and as they raised their kids, but after Papa died most of the kids had moved out. Nana's son Francis, who nobody seemed to like, had taken over the house and wouldn't leave, so Nana had packed up her things and moved in with Big Molly.

Tara thought she remembered hearing that Nana had eventually moved to Ontario and stayed with Aunt Kay. Then she might have lived with Joanie and Stan or with Doug and Elsie, but ended up at Gramma's. Nana had lived at Gramma's for as long as Tara could remember, but after Big Joe's heart attack she'd moved back to Cape Breton to live with Big Molly again.

"I don't think I can live there again," Nana said softly. "I love Rita, but you know she has problems—problems I can't help her with. And that Joe ... he is beyond description."

"Tell us what made you upset about Joe before you left there, Ma," Janey gently asked.

"He's a miser," Nana said, her voice growing stronger. "Did you know that Rita wanted me to give Joe twenty dollars to pay for the measly two-minute drive up to the hospital? After I'd already given him forty dollars a couple days before that!"

Tara was surprised to hear this. She hadn't thought Big Joe would go around asking for money, and she couldn't imagine him asking Nana for some just to drive her up to the hospital.

Nana went on. "I want Cathy to file my income tax right in front of them. I think they've got my name in as a dependent. No wonder I feel so queer, eh? Did you know he has a rash on his ankles?"

Tara almost burst out laughing at that. A rash on his ankles! What was Nana talking about?

"He's a miser, for sure," Nana went on. "Did you know when he came home with the Thanksgiving turkey it only had one wing on it? Its side was all red where a dog or some animal tore the wing off, and then Joe bought it off the man for six dollars!"

Nana sounded beside herself. Tara had never heard Nana talk this much before, let alone saying all these things about Big Joe. She'd had no idea that Nana didn't like him. She wondered if Gramma knew. *Should I ask her? Maybe I should ask Mom instead.*

"So I told Rita I wasn't going to eat one bite of that one-armed turkey and she got real mad. Anyway, she started cooking it, but by four o'clock it still wasn't done. Then Joey came in with Joe, and they were hungry, so they grilled steaks or hamburgers or something, and drank beer and brandy." Nana's rocking had stopped at this point. "I'd only had a few spoonfuls of tomato soup at twelve-thirty, so by then I was starving. But since Joe and Joey had already eaten and Rita had already had tuna and cheese or something, she wasn't hungry and didn't think to offer me anything. So I just got up out of the rocking chair and went to bed."

None of this sounded like the Gramma's house she knew, and Tara wasn't sure if she believed Nana. She loved Nana with all her heart, but she couldn't help but wonder if maybe she was exaggerating.

"Well, let's wait until we talk to Cathy, Ma. Maybe we should call her instead of waiting ten years for a letter to arrive," said Janey. "In the meantime, do you think we should just talk to Aunt Rita and see what she has to say?"

"No, no, dear, we're not going to talk about Big Joe to Rita." By the tone of her voice, Tara knew that Nana's eyes were growing wide as owl's eyes. "She thinks the sun rises and sets on that man. No. Better to talk to Cathy and tell her that I don't want to go to Rita's."

"Cathy will figure everything out, Mama," agreed Big Molly. "She always does."

Nana wasn't about to let the turkey story go. "Did you know that by the time Rita had that Thanksgiving dinner ready, it was almost six o'clock? She told me to come down to eat, but by the time I got to the table they had already prit' near finished." The squeak of the rocking chair was getting louder. "Do you know that turkey is supposed to have skin on it, Janey?" Nana asked. "Well, Rita and Joe both had turkey legs with skin on it, eh, but they only gave me two small pieces of white turkey with no skin. Do you know where my turkey skin went?"

"No, Ma, where did the turkey skin go?" asked Janey.

"To that dirty dog! That's where!"

Big Molly sighed. "OK, now, Mama, don't worry about all these things. We'll tell Cathy and she'll take care of it all for you. Janey, can you put the kettle on for another cup of tea?"

Tara had started sorting out the cards again as Janey came into the kitchen to put the kettle on.

"How are you, dear?" Janey asked as she sat down at the table, across from Tara. "I haven't seen you since I changed your diapers. How are you doin'?"

"I'm good, Janey," Tara said, putting her cards away. "My mom says to say hello, to you and to all your kids and to your husband."

"Aww, you're such a sweet thing, Tara. Just like your mom."

"Janey, can I ask you a question?"

"Sure, dear, ask me anything. I have to wait for this kettle to boil anyway."

"A few minutes ago, I heard you call Nana 'Ma,' but isn't she your grandma? Don't you call her Nana like everyone else does?"

Janey smiled softly at Tara and said, "Do you want to hear a story about me and Ma?"

Tara loved hearing stories about the family, and she was excited to hear one from Janey.

"When I was a little girl, just about the same age as you, I lived with Ma and Marlene. One day I came home from school to tell Ma that all the parents were invited for a fun event. Ma came, but once she was there I realized how much older she was than all the other moms. The next day, I asked her, 'Ma, why are all the other mothers younger than you? Why are you the oldest one?' And do you know what she said?"

Tara shook her head.

"She said, 'I'm not your mother, dear.' 'What do you mean?' I asked. 'Who is my mother?' 'Molly, from up the road, dear, she's your mother, she said.'" Janey paused. "And that's what she told me. That my mother was Molly from up the road. I was in shock. I couldn't believe it. My whole life, I'd believed that Ma was my mother and so, to this day, I still call her Ma and I call Big Molly, Molly."

Tara didn't know what to say. She wondered if her mom knew about this. *Does* anyone *know about this?*

"But don't you worry your head about it, Tara. It's alright. Molly couldn't take care of me when I was a baby, so Ma did. But you know what else? I always thought Marlene was my sister because we both lived with Ma, but then I found out that wasn't so. Marlene came from the McGillivray family so Ma wasn't her mother, either, and I'm not her sister…but me, your mom, and Marlene, we're are all cousins, in one way or another. I know it's all very confusing, isn't it? But the most important thing is that we all love each other very much, no matter where we all came from."

Janey got up from her chair and came around the table to give Tara a big hug.

"That's a lot of information for a little girl, eh? But a lot of stuff like that happened in those days, Tara, and eventually we all came back 'round and it all worked out in the end. Now, how about a hot cup of tea?"

CHAPTER NINE

Summer 1980—Back in Ontario

One minute Tara was in Cape Breton with Big Molly and her family, and the next, she was back at home with her mom in Kitchener.

Just before leaving Cape Breton, Gramma had been able to talk Nana into coming back to Ontario with her and Tara. At first Nana didn't seem comfortable with the idea, but between Janey and Big Molly talking to Cathy, and Cathy talking to Nana and Gramma, they all decided that it was for the best for Nana to go back to Stratford.

As soon as Tara woke up the morning after arriving home from Cape Breton, she quickly got out of bed to go and find her mom. She hadn't had a chance to talk to her last night because, by the time Big Joe, Gramma, and Nana had dropped her off, it was her bedtime and she was too tired from the trip to talk. But now, with so many stories and things to tell, she wanted to find her mom...and maybe ask her a couple questions, too.

Down in the perfectly clean kitchen, Tara found a crust of toast and a sip of tea had been left for her on the counter. Tara looked around and noticed that the floor was spotless, the windows were gleaming, and there was a pie cooling on the counter. It smelled like Heaven on earth. Tara's mom always spent her weekends cleaning, cooking, baking, doing laundry, and getting groceries. She worked hard all week as a bookkeeper at a transport company, and then she worked just as hard all weekend keeping the house in tip-top shape.

Tara also noticed some fabric swatches on the counter. It looked like her mom was going to change the dining room curtains again. Her mom didn't have much money, but she always liked to do her best to decorate the house nicely—and then redecorate when she got sick of it. 'Thank goodness for layaway,' she'd always say.

Tara found her mom working in the garden in the backyard, as was usual on warm and sunny summer mornings. Standing on the wooden deck at the back door of their semi-detached house, Tara could see that her mom's knees were covered in dirt, tendrils of dark hair were stuck to her face, and she was wearing large rubber boots with her old cotton shorts and T-shirt.

It was a far cry from other nights when she came home from her Mary Kay cosmetic parties.

Her mom said that being a bookkeeper didn't pay enough to make ends meet, so she'd decided to become a consultant for Mary Kay cosmetics to help with the bills. Tara knew her mom needed extra money to pay for Tara's dance lessons and summer camp, and for Ronnie's sports and activities, and the lamps, carpets, and clothes her mom was always putting on layaway. Tara loved seeing her mom all dressed up in her Mary Kay outfit—a cute skirt, satin blouse, high heels, and perfectly done hair and makeup—but this morning, her mom was in her dirty, sweaty garden outfit. Her mom called out as she walked up from the back of the yard and sat down on a deck chair. "Hi, little girl! Is it time for a break?"

"The garden looks good, Mom. Were you working on it the whole time I was away?" Tara asked, taking a seat on one of the lounge chairs.

"Yup, I worked in the garden and cleaned the house, and a couple times me and Marlene went bowling and out for drinks and stuff," she said as she took her dirty gloves off. "But besides that, I spent a lot of time thinking about you being all the way in Cape Breton."

"Mom, I had so much fun there! No wonder you talk about down home so much." Tara told her all about the adventures she and Molly Ann had picking blueberries, playing on the beach, and "running the roads" as Big Molly would say.

"I'm glad you had a nice visit. How was Nana? I didn't get much of a chance to talk to her when they dropped you off last night. How was she during the plane ride?"

"She was quiet, but her eyes were real wide. She kept saying that her ears were plugged and that her side was sore, and she kept asking when we would get to Ontario. I don't think she likes flying at all."

"No, I know she doesn't. I took her on a plane one time, when I was about sixteen years old, and she wouldn't let go of my hand for three hours. She was petrified! Anyway, how was she when she was at Big Molly's?"

"She didn't say much most of the time, but one night I could hear her talking to Janey and Big Molly and she was really upset about Big Joe."

"Yes, Janey called me and told me," she said. "She called me to talk about Mom wanting to take Nana back with her to Ontario. I told Janey that if Nana was to stay in Stratford again, I would visit often and make sure she was alright. It's probably best for Nana to stay in Stratford. It's a lot quieter and less chaotic than at Big Molly's."

"Well, I hope Nana will be OK living with Big Joe again. When Nana was talking that night, she was telling everyone about a turkey that had its wing ripped off," Tara explained. "Nana thought a dog ate the wing, and she was mad Big Joe bought it anyway."

"Honey, it's not really about a turkey, or the twenty dollars or whatever she paid Big Joe for gas. See, when Nana was a young girl she'd always wanted to be a nun. But, instead, she got married and had ten kids. She was never very happy with the life she'd ended up with. I mean, it was hard. Papa was in the mine all day and they didn't have any money; they could hardly keep all the kids clothed and fed, especially the younger ones. But I think she blamed her husband and I think, maybe, for that reason, she doesn't like most men. She's never comfortable when there's a man around. She's always suspicious and distrustful. And she worries a lot. She worries about money, about where she's going to live, and about where her stuff is. You know she moves around a lot and she spreads herself thin being here and there and everywhere."

"Why does she do that?" Tara remembered thinking about all the places Nana had lived. She'd stayed at Big Molly's, Janey's, Gramma's, and even Aunt Kay's for a while.

"I think she worries about favouring one of her kids over the other. I always thought that her kids competed for her attention, for her love, so they invite her to live with them. But, no matter what, something always goes wrong and Nana moves on to the next house. I think her kids want her to love them best."

"Does she love you, Mommy?" Tara asked, thinking that if Nana's children were competing for her love, how much was left over for Nana's grandchildren?

Her mom shifted her weight in the chair and looked out over her garden.

"When I was a little girl, I always knew I loved Nana unconditionally, even though she never loved me best. That, she gave to Janey," her mom said thoughtfully. "But I knew she loved me. She always said I was 'calm, cool, and collected.' Ha! What a great actress I was. Of course, I always strived to live up to that image for her. I hope I never failed her…I don't think I did." Her mom pulled her legs up to her chest and wrapped her arms around her knees. "I don't know why Nana couldn't, or wouldn't, show much affection. Maybe it was that her generation was taught not to show their feelings. When I was five years old and left her to come to Ontario, she'd hugged me and her body heaved with dry sobs, but no tears. I was crying buckets." Her mom turned back to Tara and smiled. "Well, I guess that sounds like a sad state of affairs, doesn't it? I probably shouldn't be telling you this stuff, it's just that I love Nana so much and if anything happens to her, I don't know what I'll do. I wonder if maybe she could live with us."

"But Gramma wants her back at her place, right?" asked Tara.

Her mom got quiet and pressed her lips together. "Yes, and Mom better take care of Nana properly; make sure she eats and takes her pills and bathes and puts fresh clothes on. It's not easy, you know, and I'm not sure how good Mom is at taking care of people. She never took much good care of me." She stood up and put her gardening gloves back on. "Anyway, I have to get back to my weeding."

"Wait, Mom. Do you think you love Nana more than you love Gramma?" Tara asked, worried. Tara loved Gramma with all her heart, but not more than she loved her mom.

"Tara, it's more complicated than that. But when I lived with Nana in Cape Breton, when I was there with her and Papa and Marlene and Janey, I was happy. Nana didn't love me the most. I knew she loved Janey more, and that was OK because I loved Janey too, but I knew Nana wanted me to stay with her. I felt so safe and protected with her, and just knowing she wanted me was all I needed. But then I went to Ontario and we moved in with that wretched Mrs. Wrenn and my whole life changed."

Tara had known Mrs. Wrenn's name would come up. It always did when her mom talked about her childhood.

"She was just so mean to me. She'd either send me upstairs by myself for hours, or she'd make me clean while her kids watched TV. She was always watching me and saying mean things about my mother. She would come upstairs to our room and look at the dust and the dirt and the cigarette ashes, and I would be so embarrassed that our place wasn't clean. She just made my life so miserable."

"Did you tell Gramma?" Tara asked. "What did she do?"

"She didn't do anything. She just told me to get along with Mrs. Wrenn, or we'd be thrown out and we had nowhere to go. So I guess, even as a young girl, I was under pressure to do what I was told and to not get into trouble or it would be my fault if we got kicked out." Tara's mom took her gloves off again and threw them onto the chair. "This is just getting me upset now. I hate that woman, and I'll never forgive her. Maybe I should be alone for a few minutes, Tara. Sorry. Why don't you run in the house and get yourself some pie?"

Once inside and eating a large slice of apple pie at the kitchen table, Tara thought about what her mom had just told her. She understood that Mrs. Wrenn had been mean to her mom, but she was surprised that after all these years her mom was still mad at her. Maybe if Tara talked to Gramma about this, Gramma could fix it somehow. Gramma always wanted everyone to get along and she didn't like when anyone was upset, so Tara was sure Gramma could make her mom feel better about Mrs. Wrenn.

———————⋅◄∞►⋅———————

A few days later, Tara's mom told her they had to drive to Stratford that afternoon. Nana was having nose bleeds, and

Gramma didn't know what to do. They got there in record time, and the car had hardly stopped before her mom jumped out and ran up the steps and into the house.

"Where is she?" she asked Gramma, looking around for Nana.

Gramma was standing in the front hall, a cigarette dangling from her shaking hand. "She's upstairs. The doctor was here and he stuffed cotton up Mama's nose to stop the bleeding. He said if it soaked through, I was to call the ambulance right away to take her to the hospital."

Running up the stairs, Tara and her mom found Nana lying down on the single bed in her room. She was pale as a ghost, and behind her thick glasses her big brown eyes were wide.

"Oh, Cathy. It wouldn't stop bleeding," Nana said, moaning. "I woke up and saw the blood on my pillow, and I got to the bathroom and held my head over the toilet and it just kept coming and coming. The toilet was filling up and I got scared, so I hollered down to Rita to call the doctor. He got here fast and stuffed all this up my poor nose."

Tara's mom sat on the bed and took Nana's hand while she inspected the cotton.

"I think it's still bleeding, Nana. Here, let me take a closer look. Yeah, this doesn't look good. Mom!" she yelled down the stairs. "How long ago did the doctor leave?"

"What's that, hun?" Gramma called back from the bottom of the stairs.

"For God's Sake, Mom, come up here. When did the doctor leave?"

"Oh, about two hours ago now, I guess." Gramma's voice sounded faint, as if she were walking back toward the front hall.

Is Gramma afraid to come upstairs to Nana's room?

"Can you please go down there, Tara, and tell her to call an ambulance right now…the blood is coming right through this stuff," her mom said in a tight voice.

Tara ran downstairs. Gramma was still standing there, but the cigarette had fallen and made a burn mark in the carpet.

"Mom wants you to call the ambulance." Tara stopped and took a closer look at her grandmother. "Are you OK, Gramma?"

Gramma nodded slowly while she dialled the big heavy phone with shaking fingers.

Tara went into the kitchen thinking that maybe Gramma needed a glass of water. On the kitchen table, beside the tea cup, was an almost empty bottle of the light-brown stuff. She wasn't sure what to do. *Should she put it away behind the couch where Gramma always put it?* She didn't even want to touch it, but somehow she didn't think her mom should see it. She was too nervous to figure out what to do, so she just got the glass of water, carefully placed it on the wooden bench beside where Gramma was sitting, and ran back upstairs.

Her mom had Nana sitting up, and had just finished putting a fresh housedress over Nana's head and was now helping her up and out of the bed.

"Do you think you can hold on to me, Nana?" her mom asked. "I'll help you down the stairs, and then we'll be ready when the ambulance gets here."

Very slowly, her mom helped Nana down the two flights of stairs to where Gramma was already holding the screen door open for the paramedics. They brought in a gurney and helped Nana lie down. Once she was secured, they whisked her down the steps and into the waiting ambulance.

"You stay here with Gramma, Tara. I'll follow Nana up to the hospital. Mom, get yourself together and take care of Tara." She threw Gramma a look that Tara had never seen before, nor wanted to see again.

After Tara closed the screen door, she found Gramma sitting at the kitchen table with her head in her hands.

"What's wrong, Gramma, are you feeling sick?" Tara patted her gently on the back.

Not looking up at Tara, Gramma answered. "Ever since I got home from Cape Breton, my head has been aching and my back is sore and I don't know...I just feel so sad."

Tara had never seen Gramma this way before. Gramma was always so fun and talkative, and loved singing and playing cards and telling stories. Today, she looked pale and tired and frail.

"Can I get you something, Gramma?" Tara felt helpless and didn't know what to do. "I can put the kettle on for you if you like?"

"That would be nice, dear. If I could just get this headache to go away, I'd feel so much better. Can you go to that cupboard there and get my ASAs, please?"

Tara plugged in the kettle, then pulled two cups down from the one cupboard and the ASAs from the other cupboard. She gave the pills to Gramma with another small glass of water, even though she knew Gramma could just swallow them dry.

"You know, I was so happy when I was down home visiting everyone," Gramma said as she waited patiently for the kettle to boil. "It was so nice to see Mama, and Big Molly and her family, and everyone else, but I felt sort of lost down there. I've been in Ontario since thirty-seven years and have only gone home every other year for two weeks, so I don't feel like I know anyone down there anymore."

Tara set the cup of tea and the Carnation on the table in front of Gramma, then sat down in front of her own cup.

"I felt real good when I saw my cousins, Marie and Marjorie. But whenever I go home to Cape Breton I think I'm going to see poor Daddy, then I realize he's dead and it makes me feel very depressed," Gramma said. "When I'm in Ontario, where I belong, I think about him but it isn't such an awful feeling as it is when I go home."

"Gramma, I know you're sad, but we're here with you now. Me, Mom, and Nana, and you'll feel better soon."

"Thank you, dear, you're such a smart girl. I've babysat lots of kids, but you're one of the smartest kids I know. Except for Junior, he's really smart," she said as she patted Tara's hand.

Normally, Tara would have laughed at that, but she felt that she should just be quiet and let Gramma talk.

"Mama used to be so happy here with me, Big Joe, and Joey, but this time around she doesn't seem happy a'tall. She's such a kind and understanding mother, it's no wonder everyone loves her, but I'm her first-born and I always thought she'd be the most comfortable with me. I thought I'd bring her up here to my place because it's always so busy at Big Molly's. I thought maybe she'd enjoy the peace and quiet. But, as soon as she got here, she started whispering about Joe and about money and paperwork and things of that nature. I've only ever asked her to pay Joe when he drives her to doctor's appointments, and I didn't think she minded. But the other day when I asked her to give him five dollars she got real quiet, gave me the money, then looked away. I don't know what I did, but things don't feel the same between us." She took a Kleenex and wiped her eyes and her nose, then fished around in her apron pocket for her pack of cigarettes. "Well, I think those pills are working now, Tara. Let's go and watch some TV while we wait for your mom to get back."

Tara's mom didn't return to the house until later that evening. She told Gramma that the doctors wanted Nana to stay overnight. They had to cauterize her nose to stop the bleeding, and they wanted to keep an eye on her. The doctors had said that once she was stable she'd be able to go home and rest, and that she shouldn't have any more issues.

They were all relieved, but they were starving so Big Joe went to pick up chicken from the Dixie Lee. The four of them ate their supper in silence before Cathy announced that she and Tara were leaving.

"Would you like to stay the night, hun?" asked Gramma. "It's a long drive back to Kitchener and you look exhausted."

"Well, yes, I feel exhausted, Mom, because that was a very serious situation with Nana. She could have bled to death, for God's sake."

"I thought she was alright," said Gramma. "I thought she was having a nice sleep. I had no idea the cotton was soaking through."

"Well, maybe you should have thought about checking on her instead of doing whatever it was that you were doing at two o'clock in the afternoon."

Gramma's eyes flitted over to the couch at the back of the room and Tara's mom followed the look.

"I thought so." She pressed her lips together and raised her left eyebrow. "Come on, Tara, we're going. Now!"

Sitting low in her seat, watching the dark world go by, Tara felt exhausted too. She was confused about Gramma and her mom, and about her mom and Nana, and about Nana and Gramma. Nothing seemed OK and she didn't know why. She loved all of them so much. Why didn't they love each other the same way? She tried to think it all through, but eventually she fell asleep and slept deeply all the way back to Kitchener.

CHAPTER TEN

Summer 1981—Time Spent with Nana

It was early July, and Tara had just arrived again at 98 Railway Avenue.

She was now seven, going on eight, years old. She'd just finished grade two, and was excited to start grade three in the fall. This was the third time Tara had been allowed to spend two weeks of her summer vacation at Gramma's house, but as much as she loved spending time with Gramma and Big Joe she was looking forward to being with Nana a lot more this time.

This past year there had been lots of worried telephone calls and letters going back and forth between Tara's mom and Nana. Nana had suffered several nose bleeds and had had to go to the hospital a few more times, but now everything seemed to be getting under control and Nana was getting used to the fact that she now lived at Gramma's.

Many times over the past several months, Tara's mom went to Stratford and picked up Nana to take her shopping for whatever it was she needed. Usually, it was a new brassier—that's what Nana called bras—socks, or a new housedress or underpants. Nothing Gramma ever got her seemed to be the right fit.

Tara's mom had told her about one time when she'd arrived in Stratford and had found Nana up in her room with all her bras lying on the bed, a sharp pair of scissors in her hand. Nana could be funny like that. None of the bras seemed to fit right for her, so she'd taken things into her own hands and "fixed" them.

"These are all too, tight, Cathy," Nana had said to Tara's mom, holding up a tattered brand-new bra. "The sides are digging into my underarms and giving me a pain, so I've been cutting them to see if they would loosen but it's still not right." And so her mom had had to go uptown to Woolworths to buy Nana another few sets of bras.

As soon as Tara stepped inside the front hall, she hugged Gramma carefully. She was always worried that she'd break one of Gramma's bones if she hugged her too tight. Tara took a few minutes to look around the house to see if there was anything new. There was often something different, like a new ceramic statuette in the china cabinet, or a new wall hanging with an Irish saying or prayer, or a framed picture placed on the floor model TV set. Today, Tara saw two huge framed portraits hung on the living room wall above Gramma's chair. One was of Jesus and the other was of the Virgin Mary. She also noticed a picture of who Gramma still called the "new" Pope—John Paul II. Gramma always said she thought he was "real handsome" and Big Joe was proud to say that the Pope was Polish, just like him.

"We got those for Mama so she can look at them when she says her prayers," Gramma told Tara. "She's still sleeping upstairs. She's been sleeping in a lot lately."

Tara looked over at Nana's rocking chair and saw on her little table a few sets of rosaries, a pile of small prayer books, and a glass dish that Tara knew was full of holy water. There was a crucifix on the wall behind her rocker, and Easter palms crossed over the doorway leading into the kitchen. Gramma went to church on Sundays, and said her prayers every day, but Nana was real religious and took being a Catholic seriously!

Besides Nana's religious things scattered about the house, most things that Tara was familiar with had not changed. That's what she loved about Gramma's house; except for a few doo dads here and there, it was always the same. Knowing what to expect made her feel comfortable—Tara wasn't fond of change, and the fact that Gramma hardly updated anything was alright with her.

"I'm so happy you're here again, Tara." Gramma gestured her to sit in the living room so they could catch up before Nana needed her lunch. "I was missing you something fierce after you left Nana's birthday party."

Back in early April, Tara, Ronnie, and their mom had gone to Nana's seventy-eighth birthday party. They had cake and presents, and had been enjoying a nice visit when suddenly her mom got mad and they'd had to leave.

Nana had been talking about her memories of birthday celebrations past, and then Gramma had brought up that on the eighteenth of April it would be Cathy's birthday. She would be thirty-one years old, but Gramma said she could remember back to the day that Cathy had been born. She talked about how the nuns had tried to take her baby away from her, but she had fought tooth and nail to keep Cathy. She kept saying over and over how proud of herself she was for fighting for her daughter.

Her mom had rolled her eyes and mumbled that she thought Gramma should have given her up to the nuns.

"Cathy, no! I wanted to keep you. I didn't want to give you away," Gramma said, her voice shaky.

"But you did, Mom. You gave me away to Nana and Papa. You didn't want me, remember?"

"Now, Cathy, Rita did the right thing having us take care of you while she looked for work and a place to live," said Nana.

Her mom had pressed her lips together so hard, her whole face had gone white. "Yes, and then she took me away from you and made me live with that witch, Mrs. Wrenn," she said, eyes narrowing to slits.

"Oh, hun! Mrs. Wrenn wasn't that bad, was she? I remember when she went to the hospital to visit you when you had Ronnie. She gave you that nice card."

Tara's mom's dark blue eyes turned black, her mouth set in a straight white line. Everyone went silent as they watched her frantically look around for her purse and keys.

"Get in the car," she'd said quietly to Tara and Ronnie.

As they were getting their coats on and heading out the door, Gramma had rushed into the front hall and said, "Hun, what did I say? Why are you running out?"

Cathy had turned to face her mother and, between clenched teeth, said, "She *did* come to the hospital to give me a card, but that meant nothing to me!" Her mom had a way of flicking her thumb and finger together, as if flicking away a disgusting bug, and she did this now. "Why didn't she understand how much I hated her? I will never forgive her as long as I live!"

And, once again, Tara had found herself holding onto her seatbelt as her mother tore out of the driveway and sped without a word all the way back to Kitchener.

"That wasn't a very nice ending to Nana's birthday party, was it," Tara said, shaking the memory of her mom's anger out of her head. "I felt bad for Mom because she was so upset, but I don't like how she yelled at you, Gramma."

Gramma shook her head. "No, it wasn't. My heart was aching for weeks after that when Cathy didn't come to see me or let you and Ronnie come for a visit. I missed her terribly during that time and I felt so bad—all on account of a misunderstanding. I thought I would just have to live with it, and pray that one day she'd come back to me." Gramma wiped her eyes and lit a cigarette. "But I couldn't let it get my nerves, Tara, because I'd hate to end up in the mental hospital and that's where I'd be if I couldn't see you three again."

Tara didn't know what to think. A mental hospital? Was Gramma being serious? Was that why she took so many pills all the time? Tara didn't really think so...she knew those pills were for headaches, flu symptoms, and sinus pain. But Gramma always seemed to have the flu or a sinus cold or some pain in her back. Come to think of it, Tara's mom took a lot of pills too. Her mom always said that things were "getting on her nerves," but Tara didn't really know what that meant.

"Well, that's enough of that kind of talk, Tara," said Gramma, interrupting Tara's thoughts. "Let's cheer up, shall we?"

The day brightened when Nana finally came downstairs. "Hello, Tara, my dear. How are you?" She squeezed Tara's hand while she took her seat at the kitchen table.

"Hi, Nana! I'm good. Did you have a good sleep?" Tara asked.

"You two just sit and have a nice chat while I get busy at the stove," Gramma said as she headed toward the refrigerator to pull out ingredients for lunch.

Soon after, Gramma set plates full of eggs, bacon, and toast in front of Nana and Tara. They liked having breakfast for lunch once in a while. Tara watched Nana say her prayers, and just as Nana was about to start eating she stopped, folded her hands in her lap, and sat quietly, staring at her plate.

"What's going on, Mama? You don't like your lunch?" Gramma asked.

Nana opened her brown eyes wide and looked all around.

"Oh, for Pete's sake, did I forget to give you a knife and fork?" asked Gramma, getting the utensils out of the drawer. "You can ask me, Mama. Don't just sit there letting your food get cold."

Tara put her hand over her mouth to try and hide her smile. It was always comical watching Nana and Gramma together. She didn't know if Nana was being serious, or just being silly on purpose to drive Gramma nuts.

Nana took her fork and started picking at her food. She stabbed at her eggs and flipped them over. Then she stopped and looked directly at Tara. With her long finger she pointed at the egg, and with her fingernail she pushed the egg white back and forth until suddenly she uncovered a round white pill. She raised her eyebrows, picked up the pill, and slowly put it in the pocket of her housedress. She nodded knowingly at Tara then quietly starting eating.

Tara smiled to herself. She knew Gramma had a hard time getting Nana to take her pills, and that often Nana would refuse them, so Gramma had started hiding the pills in Nana's food. But little did she know that Nana always fished them out and stowed them away in her housedress pockets. Tara knew Gramma would be mad if she found out, but she didn't think it was her place to tell.

After lunch, Nana asked Gramma to get the deck of cards from the cupboard.

"Do you want me to tell you your future, my dear?" Nana asked Tara, laying out the cards. As she flipped them over she told Tara that she would have a happy life, and would get married and have two kids. Tara was excited about the possibility of having her own children. She hoped she would have two little girls, and that the three of them would be best friends.

After Tara's fortune had been read, Gramma started the dishes and Nana went into the living to rock in her chair and read over her booklets. There was only one sink, and the counter beside it was so small there was nowhere for the dishes to drip dry. So, Tara grabbed a tea towel and started drying the dishes for Gramma. While she did, she looked around the kitchen and noticed a new thing on the wall above the stove.

"What's that, Gramma? Is that new?"

Following Tara's gaze, Gramma answered. "Oh, yes, my friend Katy Daly gave that to me when I was in the hospital with my broken shoulder last winter."

Tara remembered her mom telling her that Gramma had tripped going down the stairs. She had broken her shoulder and a few bones in her elbow, and she said they still pained her when the weather was rainy and damp. *Poor Gramma*, Tara thought. She had such brittle bones; she called it osteoporosis. Tara had told Gramma that she should drink more milk, but Gramma hated milk. Come to think of it, so did her mom. Tara wondered if Carnation was considered milk.

"It's an old Irish blessing," Gramma said. "'May the sun shine warm upon your face, and rains fall soft upon your fields. And until we meet again, May God hold you in the palm of His hand.' Isn't that beautiful, Tara?"

"Yes, it is," Tara agreed. "Is Katy Daly the lady we met last summer? The one who lives on Wellington Street on the way uptown?"

"That's the one! She's such a kind soul. She's a very dear person to me," Gramma said, getting back to the dishes.

"And that green-and-orange knitted thing, is it a pot holder?" Tara asked. "Did she give you that, too?"

"I can't remember now where I got that, but do you know why it's green and orange?" Gramma asked. "It's because the Catholics in Ireland are green, and those Protestants are orange. They don't get along a'tall because green—that's us—is good, and orange is bad, so they say."

Tara smiled at that. Just like Nana, Gramma, and Mom, Tara was Catholic, but her stepdad made her go to the public school instead of the Catholic school. Alpine Public and Our Lady of Grace were separated by a soccer field, and every day at recess the "Protestants," as they were called, declared war on the "Catholics," and the "Catholics" fought back with a vengeance. Tara never really knew what team she was supposed to be on, and thought her life would make a bit more sense if she'd been allowed to go to Our Lady of Grace instead of Alpine Public. She wanted to be a good Catholic like the rest of the women in her life, so she felt a bit embarrassed that she went to a public school.

Later that day, after her afternoon nap, Nana declared that her hair had gone dead-straight overnight and she needed a perm. Tara knew from the box that "perm" was short for permanent—"a process of curling hair with chemicals and rollers." Another thing Tara knew about perms was that they smelled bad! Gramma kept a few boxes of what she called "Toni's" in the cupboard, and every few months either she or Nana, or whoever was over at the time, decided they needed a Toni.

"Oh, Mama, are you sure you want a Toni right now? I was hoping to put my feet up for a bit," said Gramma, rubbing her temples.

"Rita, would you look at this hair? It's as straight as a pin," Nana said from the living room.

Without going in to look, Gramma set up the chair in the middle of the kitchen and got her plastic cape out of the closet.

She called into the living room. "C'mon then, Mama, if you want to get the perm done this afternoon!"

Slowly, Nana walked in, looked around, and found the chair. She sat down carefully then asked Tara to go to the living room and get her a stool for her feet.

Gramma mixed the stinky concoction and put the bowl aside. She took all the rollers out of the box and set them up on the counter. Then she wrapped the cape around Nana's neck and tied it at the back.

"That's too tight, Rita, are you trying to choke me?"

Sighing, Gramma re-tied the cape until Nana relaxed.

"Now, Tara dear, when I'm ready, you hand me a small roller, OK?" Gramma took a fine-toothed comb and made short, straight parts here and there in Nana's snow-white hair. "Roller."

Tara passed her the small pink-plastic roller. "Gramma, that really smells strong! Did you mix it the right way?"

"Of course, dear, I've done this hundreds of times. I can do it with my eyes closed. Roller." She held her hand out.

After about a half an hour, Nana's whole head was covered in pink rollers, and her scalp was starting to look pink too.

"Now for the cap," Gramma said. "Tara, can you get the cap out of the box for me?"

Once Nana had the cap on, she had to sit there for two hours. Tara knew there'd be a lot of tea drinking going on, and even though she loved hearing Gramma and Nana talk she wondered if she could go to the Handy to get some candy. Gramma gave her two dollars and told her to be careful crossing the street.

"You know those crazy drivers go way too fast around that bend, Tara, so make sure you look both ways before you cross," said Gramma, putting her wallet back in her purse.

When Tara got back to the house with her brown bag full of candy, Gramma and Nana were nowhere to be found. She called their names, but there was no answer. She listened carefully and thought she could hear voices coming from Nana's room upstairs. She went up to investigate, and she couldn't believe what she saw.

There was Nana sitting on her bed, with a large tub of Vaseline in her lap, and Gramma furiously pacing up and down the room, smoking a cigarette.

"Mama, what have you done?" Gramma stopped pacing and put her hands on her hips.

"You did something wrong with that chemical mixture, Rita. I told you it was burning the skin right off my head, and when I took the rollers out the curls looked real weird."

"But, Mama, you only had the chemical on for thirty minutes. The Toni box says you need to have it on for two hours!"

"I don't care what the box said, Rita, it was burning me."

"So, you decided to lather your whole head with Vaseline??" said Gramma, putting her cigarette out in the ashtray she'd found.

Tara took a closer look at Nana and yes, it was true. She had clumps of thick, greasy Vaseline all through her hair. Tara hid her laughter behind a cough. *Oh my God*, she thought. *What's going on here?*

"The curls were no good, Rita, and my scalp hurt so I soothed it with a little Vaseline."

"A *little* Vaseline? Mama, the whole tub's almost gone!"

For the next forty-five minutes, Gramma had Nana bent over the bathtub, trying desperately to wash the thick goo out of Nana's hair. Gramma used all the Herbal Essences she had— she even tried Sunlight, but nothing was working.

With Gramma's back almost broken, and Nana's knees ready to give out, Gramma finally said, "I give up. I can't do this anymore. Mama, put this towel on your head and go sit in your room until your hair is dry, or as dry as it can get with all that Vaseline in it. I'm going down to make us tea, and you just come down when you're ready."

Back on her bed, Nana sat with her head in a damp towel, her eyes as big as saucers and her hands folded in her lap. "That Rita, she doesn't know how to give a Toni," she said, shaking her head from side to side. "Next time I'll ask Cathy to do it."

Tara giggled to herself all the way down the stairs. *Poor Gramma*, she thought, *she tries so hard to please Nana, but Nana is so silly.* She hoped Gramma could forget her frustration and see how funny it all was.

———————•⟨∞⟩•———————

That night, Tara asked if she could sleep with Nana. Nana said that all her life some child was sleeping with her, whether it was one of her own kids, Janey and Marlene, or one of Big Molly's crew, and so Tara should be no different.

Tara went into the bathroom and got her nighty on and brushed her teeth. She was glad that when she flushed the toilet she would only have to run into Nana's room and not all the way down the stairs. She wondered what Nana thought of those monsters at the top of the house being so close to her room.

"C'mon now, my dear, get under the bedclothes before you catch a draft," Nana said. "Now, before we go to sleep, we have to say our prayers."

Tara was worried because she didn't say *actual* prayers before she went to bed at home, she just said that she loved God and her mom and prayed for Him to please keep everyone safe. Nana was serious about her prayers, so Tara would have to listen carefully.

"Don't you worry, my dear, you can repeat after me. Ready?"

Nana had a soft, raspy voice and she was often hard to understand. Between her voice, her accent, and just the fact that she spoke quietly, Tara found it hard to keep up.

"O my God, at the end of this day I thank You most heartily for all the graces I have received from You," Nana began.

"O my G—" Tara started to repeat the words.

"I am sorry that I have not made a better use of them. I am sorry for all the sins I have committed against You," Nana went on.

"I am sorry—" Tara repeated, but Nana wasn't waiting for her to finish before she went on to the next line.

"Forgive me, O my God, and graciously protect me this night."

"Nana, can you slow down at bit?" Tara asked.

Nana paused for a moment, but started again at the exact same pace. "Blessed Virgin Mary, my dear heavenly mother, take me under your protection. St. Joseph, my dear Guardian Angel. And all you saints of God, pray for me."

Tara decided it was best to just be quiet and listen.

"Sweet Jesus, have pity on all poor sinners, and save them from hell. Have mercy on their suffering souls in purgatory. Amen," Nana finished.

"Amen," repeated Tara.

"Bless yourself now, my dear, and go to sleep," said Nana. And with that, Nana turned off the lamp beside her bed, rolled over, and started snoring.

Tara smiled in the darkness. She felt very lucky to be able to sleep with Nana in her warm bed, and as she did with both her mom and Gramma, she felt safe and secure and loved.

CHAPTER ELEVEN

Summer 1982—A Day in the Park

It was late summer, and Tara couldn't believe how quickly a year had gone by.

Last fall, she had started grade three when she was seven years old, and now she was eight years old and ready for grade four! Tara was feeling very grown up, being eight years old. She had been a competitive dancer for a few years now, and this summer had been her fourth year at summer camp. She'd felt especially grown up when she got the chicken pox and her mom had had to leave her at home during the day while she went to work. Although the itching drove her crazy, Tara had been happy to spend the last days of June in the coolness of their rec room, watching her favourite movies and hanging out with her dogs and cats.

This past year, Tara's mom had done a lot of travelling between Kitchener and Stratford because both Gramma and Nana had been in the hospital at different times. Nana had had a bladder infection and many more bouts of nose bleeds, and poor Gramma had broken her hip. She'd said the osteoporosis was to blame. She had fragile bones, and even if she simply slipped, something would break. And she still suffered with sinus headaches and back pain, and had gotten pneumonia again over the winter.

Instead of going to Stratford for Nana's birthday in April, they'd gone to celebrate Gramma's fifty-ninth birthday in early June. Gramma had seemed so happy at her party. She was a very kind and giving person, and didn't need a lot of fuss, but she loved when her family and friends made a big deal for her birthday. She would giggle and clap her hands and wrap her arms around herself as if she was a little girl. When it was Gramma's birthday, Tara couldn't help but be happy too.

"I don't ask for anything for my birthday, as long as I have a good time and we're all together," Gramma had said. "That's better than all the gifts in the world. All I want is for everyone to love each other. That would make me happier than anything."

But, as Gramma would also always say, "One minute you're right as rain, and the next minute you're so sad you don't know what to do." In July, Gramma had gotten the news that her sister Joanie's daughter, Theresa, had died in a car crash. She'd been only twenty-three years old, and had left behind a husband and a five-year-old son.

"Theresa was loved by everyone," Gramma had explained to Tara during one of their telephone conversations. "But God took her, Tara. Why, I don't know. We're not to question God's will so I guess He took her for a reason, but I still can't get it through my head that Theresa's gone. Her casket was closed, you know, and just her picture was nearby. I feel so sorry for poor Joanie and Stan. I don't think they believe it, either. It will take a long time for us to get over this. They say time heals, but for now we are numb from the shock."

Because Gramma had been so depressed about Theresa, Tara's summer visit was postponed to August. It was hard to wait until then to go to Stratford, but Tara understood that Gramma was too sad to have company.

But now that August *had* arrived, Tara quickly got right back into the swing of things. She arrived at Gramma's late Friday afternoon, and after she'd said goodbye to her mom, Big Joe had taken her hand and led her to the kitchen.

"Look. Look here, Tara. I get you all your favourites." He chuckled as he pointed to all the items inside the fridge. There was yogurt, cottage cheese, chocolate milk, and in the freezer, ice cream and popsicles.

"How do you know that I love all these things, Big Joe?" Tara asked, trying to decide which item she would eat first.

"I know." He tapped the side of his head. "I know."

"If I ate any of that, I would be sick as a dog," said Gramma. "All that dairy would give me heartburn, I need a Tums just looking at it! Well, anyway, should we order Dixie Lee for supper?"

As usual, the four of them—Nana loved the Dixie Lee, too—ate in the living room at TV trays as they watched the evening news. Tara didn't like watching the news because she couldn't understand what they were going on about, and she and Gramma couldn't talk because Big Joe was trying to listen. Nana couldn't hear much, so she just rocked in her chair and stared at the TV.

"Gramma, what are they…?"

"Be qui'! Be qui'," Big Joe said from the back of the room.

He was very serious when the news was on, so Tara didn't let him see her smile at his thick accent. She set her face back to serious because when Big Joe was watching the news she knew it was better to just eat and "be qui!'"

Once the news was over, Nana went to bed and Big Joe went out to the Legion to play darts. Tara and Gramma watched *Falcon Crest* until it was time for bed. Tara was already looking forward to tomorrow night, when they could watch *The Lawrence Welk Show* and Sunday when *Dallas* came on.

Tara was getting used to the routine at Gramma's. On Saturday mornings she'd have breakfast with Nana, then watch cartoons in the mornings and sports in the afternoons. But she and Gramma would never know the score because as soon as the sports came on, the TV went off. Then, if the weather was nice, the day would consist of playing outside, helping Big Joe in the garden, sitting on the porch with Nana, or walking uptown with Gramma. During rainy weather, Tara, Gramma, and Nana would listen to records, look at the photo albums, or dance and sing, and play cards in the kitchen.

During the week, Big Joe went to work very early in the morning, so Gramma woke up at five o'clock to give him breakfast and see him off to work. Then she'd do the dishes, write in her diary, file her nails, and have a tea. After Gramma had given Tara and Nana their breakfast, Nana would go back upstairs for a nap, and Tara and Gramma would settle in to watch hour after hour of soap operas. After Tara ate Kraft

Dinner or a grilled cheese in front of their noon-time soap, she'd head outside to play with Ginger, or would go to the Handy or to the park.

While Tara and Gramma stuck to their regular routine, Nana would do the same: rock in her chair, say her prayers, stick out her false teeth, or tell fortunes with cards or tea leaves.

Joey would go to work every day, and then hang out with his friends from down the street all evening. He had a lot of good friends, and they'd often drop in for a quick visit before they went off to the pub uptown or to a party somewhere. He wasn't usually around for supper, or any of the fun things Tara and Gramma did together, and Tara only ever really saw him when he came downstairs to eat before leaving again.

⁓

This particular morning, the sun was shining and the skies were blue, and Tara thought it would be a perfect day to go to Dufferin Park. Now that she was eight years old, she was allowed to go by herself.

"Alright, now you be careful, Tara. Do you remember how to get there?" Gramma asked.

"Yup! I just go down Railway Avenue to the first street and turn left," Tara said, proud that she remembered. "Then, I go up two blocks and turn right and the park's right there."

"That's right, and if anyone bothers you or you get hurt, you run back here as fast as you can," said Gramma.

Tara didn't feel nervous about going to the park by herself. Because Ronnie was five years older than her, she sometimes felt like an only child and had had to learn to play by herself and be independent. At home, she was allowed to play in the forest out behind their backyard. She would pack a picnic lunch for herself and wander through the forest, which went on and on until it ended at the bottom of a steep hill. At the top of the hill there was a field that led to what they called Mount Trashmore, which was actually the old city dump that the kids used as a tobogganing hill in the winter. When it was time for her picnics, Tara would find an old stump and sit quietly for long periods of time. She would secretly hope that, if she sang softly enough, all the woodland animals would come and sit next to her, just as if she were Snow White. And just like Snow White, she loved animals of all kinds: cats, dogs, squirrels, rabbits, and even the ground hogs they'd find in their gardens.

Playing in the forest at home was fun, but she loved going to Dufferin Park here in Stratford because there were always lots of kids to meet. Tara was a bit shy sometimes, but she usually found someone she could play with.

She walked up and down the few streets that brought her to the park. First, she checked out the ball diamond. She knew there would be a game later that afternoon, and it was always exciting because people would come from all over to sit in the stands and cheer on their team. There was a concession stand there, too, where they could buy a bottle of pop and a bag of chips to snack on while spending hours watching the game.

But nothing was going on there yet, so Tara made her way over to the arena. The neatest thing about the arena was that, even in the middle of summer, there was always a big pile of snow just outside the doors. Tara knew that a machine cleaned off the top of the ice and when the machine dumped what it gathered into a pile, the pile turned into snow. She climbed up on the pile and sat for a few minutes, feeling the cold snow with her warm hands. When her bum started to get damp, she climbed down again.

She looked across the field at the playground, and noticed a few kids were already on the metal slide and the swings. On one side of the playground were a couple of wooden seesaws beside a set of monkey bars, and on the other side was a big sandbox, large enough for twenty kids to play in at one time. Beside the sandbox were three metal horses kids could sit on and sway back and forth. One was yellow, one was blue, and one was red. Tara loved the horses because if you could sway hard enough, you felt like you were flying. It felt just as if she were on Pegasus from one of her favourite TV shows, *The Mighty Hercules*.

On the far side of the playground was the rusty, faded merry-go-round. That's where all the fun happened. When it was stopped, all the kids would load themselves onto the circular platform, gripping the bars as tight as they could. You could stand and try to stay on, but if you wanted to stay on longer you had to sit on the platform and wrap your arms and legs around a pole. Then the other kids, usually two or three of them, would stand in the dirt and pull the bars to make the merry-go-round spin. The faster it went, the harder it was to hold on. Around and around you'd go until you'd start feeling yourself being pulled toward the dirt. Slowly, your sweaty hands would loosen their grip and you'd start sliding across the metal floor, unable to grab at anything to hold on to. The kids who were pulling would see that you were helpless so they would pull harder and harder, and faster and faster, until—whoop!— there you'd go, flying off the merry-go-round into the dust and dirt. It was important to make sure you rolled away from the spinning metal monster, because otherwise you'd whack your face on the spinning rusty metal or another poor kid would kick you in the head while their body flew through the air to join you in the dirt.

Before Tara made her way over to where the kids were playing, she took a walk around the big blue water tower that stood not too far away from the park. Tara wondered if she could somehow climb the tower. She walked all the way around, inspecting the foot of the tower to see if she could make it up to the ladder that started about halfway up. *How do the maintenance men do it? There must be a way.* She stepped up to the first level, where big bolts secured the tower to the base. She stepped over the first giant bolt, walked a few steps, and then stepped over the next one. On and on she went, until she made it back to where she started. The whole time she'd looked up to see where she could start climbing, but all she could see was the smooth outside of the tower and nothing to grab hold of. Maybe she would ask Joey if he knew how to climb up.

Tara felt dizzy from walking around and around the tower, so she decided to lie down on the warm green grass and look up at the sky. The sky was light blue, with only a few puffy clouds floating slowly across it. A soft breeze came up and the sun hid for a few moments, but then the breeze continued and the sun again peeked its face out from behind the clouds.

"Peek-a-boo," Tara said, whispering to the warm sun. "I see you."

The sun was warm on her face, and the breeze blew her shoulder-length hair back from her face. She closed her eyes and smiled as she let the heat of the sun tan her skin. *I could fall asleep here*, she thought. As she relaxed, her mind went to the new friends she was hoping to meet today, and like the slow-moving clouds, her thoughts drifted over to her mom.

Tara remembered her mom saying that she hadn't had any friends when she was growing up. Tara couldn't understand how her mom couldn't have had any friends. Tara had many friends at home: friends from school, friends who were neighbours that she played with every day, and friends from summer camp and dance class. She did remember her mom saying that the only real friend she'd had was the little girl in the mirror. Tara understood that it had only been her mom's own reflection and not a real girl, but she thought the idea of the little girl in the mirror was the saddest thing she'd ever heard. Imagine having only your reflection to tell all your thoughts and feelings to.

"Well, I couldn't tell anyone at school about my miserable life," her mom would say. "I was too embarrassed to share how unhappy I was, and it was hard for me to see all the other kids playing and laughing so easily, as if they didn't have a care in the world. My whole world was rotten—it was hard for me to feel enough joy to make myself smile or laugh. Anyway, you're

lucky, Tara. You've always been able to make friends easily. I
wish I was more like you when I was little."

Tara didn't know how to feel about this. She wanted her
mom to make friends on her own. Tara thought her mom was
funny and smart, and she spent a lot of her free time doing nice
things for people—it should be easy for her to have a good
friend. But every time someone came into her mom's life and
wanted to get close to her, she would always find something
wrong with them. They would do or say something to hurt her
feelings, and she wouldn't be able to get over it. As soon as her
mom felt hurt she would flick her fingers and say, "I'm done
with them."

Tara felt this was why her mom spent most of her time with
Aunt Marlene. They didn't always agree on everything, but they
had a certain kind of easy way with each other that made them
both comfortable. Maybe it was because they'd spent so much
of their early lives together in Cape Breton at Nana's house, or
maybe it was because they'd both been raised by Nana knowing
that Nana wasn't actually their mother. Tara's mom and Aunt
Marlene had a special bond, and they trusted each other with
all their hearts.

It occurred to her now that maybe that was why her mom
thought it was important to help who she called her "old people."
Her old people were those she met when she volunteered at
senior's centres and retirement homes. She was always making
them soup, picking up their prescriptions, cleaning or painting
their places, celebrating their birthdays with cakes and cards, or
helping them with important paperwork. She said they

appreciated her, and she liked that she could help them without expecting anything in return. They couldn't really do anything for her anyway, she'd say, and because she had no expectations from them, she didn't get her feelings hurt.

Whenever her mom's friends or her family tried to do things for her, she would narrow her eyes and say that she wondered what they were up to—as if she didn't trust them. Tara didn't really understand all of this. She just wished her mom had a good friend that she could love and trust and have fun with.

Suddenly, a big cloud covered the sun and cooled her skin. Tara's thoughts moved away from her mom and the little girl in the mirror and she jumped up, worried that all the kids would be gone before she'd had a chance to make a new friend. She headed away from the water tower and over to the park.

"Hi, my name's Tara," she said, introducing herself to a blond-haired girl and her friend who were playing in the sandbox. "Do you want to play?"

"Sure! Should we go on the merry-go-round?" asked the girl.

Not feeling like getting a mouthful of dirt today, Tara said, "How about we go on the swings first?"

They played first on the swings and then on the slide, and eventually spent a few hours in the sandbox making houses and roads for make-believe people to go around on. After several hours with the two girls, Tara noticed that the sun was going down. *That must mean it's close to supper*, Tara thought, and knew she'd better head back to Gramma's before she and Big Joe started worrying about her.

She stood up and dusted herself off and said goodbye to her friends. She began to head home when she saw a familiar man walking toward her. It was Big Joe. *Uh oh*, she thought, *I hope he's not mad.*

But when she got closer to him, she saw that he had a big smile on his red-cheeked face.

"You not coming home anymore?" he asked. "You almost miss supper."

"Oh, Big Joe! I'm surprised it's so late. I met two new friends and we played all day."

"That's OK, you having fun." Big Joe put his warm hand on her shoulder. "Let's get back to Gramma before she worry."

They walked home together, and Tara chatted about all the fun she'd had at the park. Big Joe didn't say much. He just smiled and nodded. Back at the house, Gramma was waiting on the porch.

"Tara, I was worried! I didn't think you were ever coming back so I had to send Big Joe to go and find you." She held the screen door open.

"I'm sorry, Gramma. Next time I'll ask someone for the time," Tara said, making her way past Gramma and into the front hall.

"OK, well, supper's ready. Just go wash your hands before we eat," Gramma said. "Actually, looking at you and all that dust, I'd say you're going to have a bath right after supper. Your hair is full of sand."

Tara felt that maybe her shorts were full of sand, too.

After supper, Big Joe went out to meet his friends, and Nana was having a nap, so it was just Tara and Gramma up in the bathroom getting ready for Tara's bath.

"OK, dear, this tub is ready when you are," Gramma said as she set out a towel and a clean nighty.

Tara eased herself into the warm water. At first it felt lovely, but soon she felt something hurting her bum and legs.

"Ouch, Gramma, what's in the water?"

"What do you mean?" Gramma swirled the water around with her hand. "There's nothing in the water."

"Yes, something's itching me!" Tara squirmed in the tub.

"Here let me put some of this nice bath soap in and see if that softens the water." Gramma reached for the plastic bottle on the side of the tub.

"No, that's not helping," said Tara. "Ouch! Can I get out?"

"You just got in," said Gramma as she put the bottle of bath soap away and grabbed the Herbal Essences. "Here, let's quickly get your hair washed and then you can get out."

Reluctantly, Tara leaned all the way back and put her hair in the water, but then her whole back started getting itchy. "Quick, quick, finish washing it, Gramma!"

Once Gramma rinsed her hair, Tara stood up while Gramma held a towel open and wrapped it around her. Tara instantly felt better. She turned around to look at the water and there, covering the whole bottom of the white tub, was a thick layer of sand.

"Oh, Gramma. That's what was itching me." Tara laughed. "Sandbox sand!"

"My Lord! Well, you must have spent more time in that sandbox than you should have, you silly goose!"

After Tara was all dried off and in her nighty, they went back downstairs and settled into their usual spots for some nighttime

TV. But, before their show started, Tara wanted to ask Gramma about her mom and why it was hard for her to make friends.

"Gramma, today at the park I made two new friends, and it was easy. I just went up to them and asked them to play and then we had a lot of fun. I might see them again tomorrow."

"That's good, dear, I'm glad you met some nice girls." Gramma put her legs up on her stool and lit a cigarette.

"I was thinking about how mom doesn't have friends like I do. Do you know why that is?" Tara asked.

Exhaling smoke toward the ceiling, Gramma said, "I think your mom used to have friends when she was young. She loved her friend Anne Gorman, and she used to play with a girl named Elaine, and she always played with Kenny and Susan Wrenn, the two kids we lived with for a while."

Tara remembered her mom mentioning Kenny and Susan. They were Mrs. Wrenn's adopted children. Tara didn't think her mom had liked them that much. Well, she may have liked Susan, but she'd been a lot younger than her, and her mom had said that Kenny was hard to get along with. "But, really, with a mother like Mrs. Wrenn," Tara remembered her mom saying, "how could any child she raised be easy to get along with?"

"I don't think Mom liked playing with them, Gramma," Tara said. "She said her best friend was the little girl in the mirror."

"Yes, I remember her talking to herself in the mirror," said Gramma, "but surely that wasn't her only friend?"

"Was Mrs. Wrenn really mean to her, Gramma? Mom always says that Mrs. Wrenn was a witch and that she ruined her childhood."

"Well, since the last time you asked me about this, I've been thinking back and I don't remember Mrs. Wrenn hitting your mom or yelling at her, and if she did, I would have put my foot down," said Gramma, putting her cigarette out in the ashtray. "But, you see, I was working hard at the Laundry so I could pay our rent, and buy groceries and clothes. I didn't have any help, you know, nothing from the government or from anyone else. And every month I sent money home to Mama and Papa. I know you already know this, but I didn't have a husband. I had to do everything by myself: work, take care of your mom, clean and do laundry, and make supper. Nothing was easy for me. So, when your mom used to complain when I got home from work, it was hard to take what she was saying to heart. I had sore feet, I was starving, and I was exhausted. And she was just complaining about her babysitter. I don't want to sound mean, or sound like I didn't care, but I just don't think Mrs. Wrenn was that bad and I can't understand why Cathy is so mad about it all the time. I was just doing my best under the circumstances."

"Did you ever tell Mom all of that, Gramma?" Tara asked.

"I think I have tried to tell her, Tara, but I don't think she wants to listen to me." Gramma rubbed her temples. "She just gets real mad before I can explain anything."

"Maybe it's because she wants you to listen to her stories of how mean Mrs. Wrenn was and then you can say you feel bad. Maybe she thinks you don't believe her?"

"Well, maybe I don't then, I guess. I just can't believe that things were that bad." Gramma stood up and went to turn on the TV. "Let's just watch a show. I'm getting an awful headache."

Tara felt frustrated. She was hoping that Gramma would be able to make her mom feel better about Mrs. Wrenn, but now she wondered if Gramma didn't know how to. Tara shook her head and took a deep breath, because she knew if her mother was here right now, and could hear everything Gramma was saying, she'd be furious. Tara wished she could just erase Mrs. Wrenn from her mom's memory. Back at home, there were lots of times when her mom was happy—singing while she cleaned, humming while she baked, or smiling while she gardened—but as soon as there was any talk about her childhood, Gramma, Stratford, or any people in her life who she felt had hurt her, she would clam up and stop talking. Then, when she *did* talk again, it was always about Mrs. Wrenn.

Could Mrs. Wrenn really be to blame for all the hurt and disappointment her mom felt about her life? How could one woman, from so long ago, have so much power?

Tara was getting really sick of Mrs. Wrenn.

———— ◆◄∞►◆ ————

Lying on her couch that night, just before she fell asleep, Tara thought about the time just after she'd come home from Stratford last summer.

She'd wanted to play at her neighbourhood park which was at the base of a six-story apartment building just up the road from their house. She'd rode her bicycle there but the park had been empty, so she'd sat on the swing for a while hoping someone would come along. Suddenly, a girl and her little brother walked over to the swing set. The girl was about her age but didn't look very friendly, so Tara had started swinging.

"Hey, give me that swing," the girl said.

Tara responded quietly. "There's two other swings, take one of those."

"No. I want yours. Now get off it and give it to me." The girl stood there with her hands on her hips.

Tara hadn't known what this girl was all about, but there was no way she was getting off the swing. She pumped her legs harder and swung up over the girl's head.

"You better hope you can swing forever because as soon as you stop I'm going to beat you," said the girl.

Tara couldn't believe it. *What the heck? Who is this girl?* But her legs had gotten tired and now she was worried that she wouldn't be able to swing for much longer, so she let herself slow down. When she'd got low enough, the girl said to her brother, "Hit her! Hit her in the legs!"

Tara had been wearing shorts that day and so, when the boy slapped her, it stung her exposed skin.

"Hit her again! Hit her harder!" The girl had yelled.

Using all her might, Tara pumped her legs as hard as she could and again soared up and over the kids' heads. The girl had seemed like she was growing impatient waiting for Tara to slow down again, so she'd looked around and saw Tara's bike leaning up against the wall of the apartment building.

"That's OK, I'll just take your bike."

So, while Tara swung furiously to keep away from the little brother's slapping hands, the girl took Tara's bike and rode it toward the back of the building. The brother then ran after her.

Tara's heart raced. She couldn't believe they'd taken her bike! Her mom was going to kill her. Confident they weren't making their way back to the park, Tara had slowed down, jumped off the swing, and ran home as fast as she could.

Breathlessly, she'd relayed the whole story to her mom but all her mom had said was, "Show me where this girl is."

They'd walked quickly back to the park and found it was still empty.

"They're around the back of the apartment building," Tara said, pointing in the direction the kids had taken off.

They'd found the girl at the far wall, sitting on the bike. But as soon as the girl saw Tara's mother, she got off the bike. Tara ran over to grab it before it fell to the ground.

Tara's mom had walked right up to the girl, grabbed her by the collar of her shirt, and pushed her up against the wall. "If you ever, EVER, touch my daughter or her bike again, I swear to God that I will find you and I will beat the living daylights out of you. I will take you somewhere where no one will hear you scream and I will beat you, do you understand?"

Without waiting for an answer she'd let go of the girl, walked back to Tara and her bike, and the two of them walked home.

Tara had been stunned, but at the same time she'd felt so proud of her mom. She'd thought that maybe her mom might get in trouble for threatening to beat the girl, but it had been exactly what that girl deserved. Tara had wanted to clap and cheer for her mom, but her mom had just gone into the house and hadn't said another word about it.

Tara wondered if her mom could be that vicious and determined to stick up for Tara back then, then why couldn't she stick up for herself now?

Mrs. Wrenn wasn't dead, after all. She just lived up the street from Gramma's, close to the train station. Why didn't her mom just march over there one day, grab Mrs. Wrenn by the collar, and shake her until she apologized? Why didn't her mom scream at Mrs. Wrenn for all the awful things she'd done and for how she'd made little Cathy's life so miserable?

Her mom wasn't a helpless kid anymore. She was an adult who could demand an apology, so why didn't she do something to take away the horrible feelings she had about Mrs. Wrenn?

CHAPTER TWELVE

Summer 1982—Records, Music, and Stories

Tara had been allowed to sleep with Nana again last night, but it was morning now and the sunlight was streaming in through the window. She stayed in bed for a few minutes, thinking about Nana and how happy she was to be with her, but she was getting hungry for breakfast so she slowly got out of bed. Without waking Nana, she tiptoed downstairs to see what Gramma was up to.

"Good morning, Gramma," said Tara as she made her way into the kitchen.

"Oh, Tara! You scared the living daylights out of me. I didn't hear you come down the stairs," Gramma said as she put a few slices of bread in the toaster. "Toast and honey, dear?"

"Yes, please. Sorry for scaring you, but I was trying to be quiet so that I didn't wake Nana up. She's sleeping like a log. Anyway, I noticed, coming down the stairs, that you have a few new plants on the window sill."

"Oh, yes, my African Violets. Aren't they beautiful? Did you know that all plants and flowers like when you talk to them?" asked Gramma, getting the honey out of the cupboard.

"No, I've never heard that," said Tara. "Are you sure?"

"Oh, yes. When you water them, you can ask them about their day and tell them that they're beautiful and they'll flower right before your eyes."

"I want to try that, Gramma! Do your African Violets need water now?"

"Why, sure they do." Gramma rummaged around under the kitchen sink. "Here's the watering can. Just give them a tiny bit, you don't want to drown them."

Tara filled up the watering can and then crept back up the stairs until she was level with the window sill. It was high up, but if she reached onto her tippy toes, she could water the plants without spilling anything.

"Hello, little violets," she said. "How are you today? You sure are pretty."

They didn't flower right before her eyes, but they looked happy to have a drink.

After Tara had watered the plants, she turned to face the long mirror that hung on the wall at the bottom of the stairs. Tara loved this mirror because every time she came down the stairs she could see her whole self and so she'd do a couple jazz kicks, or pretend she was a ballerina and point her toes, or act like she was a model and pose for the camera. Smiling back at her reflection, she noticed that her hair was all tangled and her nighty was wrinkled. She'd better put her shorts and T-shirt on, and get ready for the day.

"Your toast is ready, Tara," Gramma said, hollering from the kitchen.

After Tara ate her breakfast, she went to where Nana's rocking chair sat near the record player in the back part of the living room. Even though it wasn't a rainy day, she decided to flip through the albums to see what they could listen to.

She was sitting on the floor with the pile of records, absently using her foot to rock Nana's chair back and forth, when she heard Nana slowly making her way down the stairs.

"Hi, Mama, I'll get you a hot cup of tea," said Gramma, yelling from the kitchen. "You just sit in your chair with Tara and I'll be there in a jiff."

"Thanks, dear," Nana said as she came into the living room. "Oh, Lord, Tara! Don't do that, my dear!"

Tara looked up at Nana. "Don't do what, Nana?"

"Don't you know that it's bad luck to rock a chair when no one's in it? Oh, yes! That's just asking for a bad spirit or ghost or something to sit there. No, no, no. Don't rock a chair when there's no one in it, that's 'a for sure'."

"Sorry, Nana." Tara smiled. "Here, I've stopped it. You can sit down now. Can I get you something?"

"Yes, my dear. My side is painin' again." She eased herself into her chair. "Can you please plug in my heating pad?"

Once Nana had her heating pad warmed up and placed on her side, and a hot cup of tea placed on the table beside her, she settled down and relaxed. After a few minutes, she called out in her soft voice. "Is the toast prit' near ready, Rita?"

"Yes, Mama, I'll be right there," Gramma said from the kitchen, sounding exasperated.

"Tara, can you hand me that mirror there?" asked Nana while she waited. "The one on the coffee table?"

Tara passed Nana the handheld mirror she always kept nearby. Nana was a simple woman for the most part, but she was often quite concerned about the lack of colour in her cheeks.

"Good Lord, what a sight," she said, staring at her pale reflection in the mirror. "My God, Tara. Would you look at that!" She rolled her eyes and shook her head. "Rita, can you bring me the compact?"

"I'll get it, Nana." Tara jumped up and went into the kitchen to look in the drawer beside the utensils. She found the powdered rouge and brought it back to the living room.

"Thanks, my dear," said Nana. "I'll just put a little here and there." She patted a large amount of powdered rouge onto her cheeks.

Nana definitely didn't look pale anymore. Tara thought the rouge made her look a Raggedy Ann doll.

"Oh, now that's better, isn't it?" Nana asked, staring at Tara with her big brown eyes.

Tara didn't know if she was being serious or not. Then Nana raised her eyebrows up and down a few times so Tara knew she was just being silly.

"You're so funny, Nana. Here, let me take some of that off so you look more natural." Tara grabbed a tissue and gently wiped away most of the rouge. When she was finished, she handed the mirror back to Nana.

"Well, my, my! That looks better, doesn't it?" Nana asked. "Thank you, my dear. Now, why don't you get a few candies for yourself from that dish there."

Tara knew what Nana was referring to, but the dish the candies were in wasn't a dish at all. It was a large wooden bowl carved in the shape of a walnut, and it sat on the coffee table. She thought it was neat because it had a lid so you could open the walnut, and inside there was always a bunch of candies. They weren't Tara's favourite candies, though. They were brown and sticky, and they always seemed to have a thin layer of dust on them.

Oh well, a candy is a candy, so Tara took a small handful and popped them into her mouth. Tara knew Nana had Scotch mints upstairs in her room, so maybe later Nana would let her have a few of those too.

"Alright, here we go, hot toast with peanut butter and jam," Gramma said as she cleared the table and set down a saucer of toast. "What record did you choose for today, Tara?" she asked, taking a seat in her chair and putting her feet up.

Tara held up Bing Crosby. "How about this one?"

"Oh, my, yes. Play "Too-Ra-Loo-Ra-Loo-Ral." We love that one," Gramma said smiling.

Both Gramma and Nana closed their eyes and listened quietly. The two of them weren't often quiet at the same time, so Tara took the opportunity to study both their faces. She knew, from hearing stories over and over again that Nana's family were both Irish and Scottish—her parents' surnames were Hanrahan and MacIsaac. Nana's husband's family, Papa's father and all their ancestors, the Barrons, had come from Ireland.

Papa's mother's family were descended from the Mi'kmaq— they were the Doucettes from a few different areas in Ingonish.

Some of Gramma's siblings looked like the Barrons, while some looked more like the Doucettes. But, in general, Gramma's family—all ten siblings—identified with their parents' Irish ancestry.

They all loved Irish music, food, and culture, and they were serious Catholics who adored Jesus, the saints, and mostly, the Virgin Mary. Nana always chose to pray to the Virgin. She felt that men were somewhat useless. Not Jesus, though, no—but most other men.

"Aww…that was beautiful," said Gramma. "Now play "Harrigan," please. I bet you I know all the words."

And she did! Gramma sang the whole song and Nana and Tara laughed and clapped, shouting HARRIGAN at the end.

"How do you like them apples?" Gramma asking, laughing too.

Tara loved when Gramma was happy like this. She knew so many songs and loved singing. Her voice was a bit shaky at times, but Tara could tell she must have been a pretty good singer when she was young.

"Find another song, would you dear," said Gramma. She glanced at the coffee table. "Look, Mama. You have some mail here that you should take a look at." She went to the kitchen to get the metal letter opener.

"It's from The Sisters of the Precious Blood. I was hoping to hear from them soon," said Nana. She took the metal opener from Gramma, and sliced open the top of the envelope.

As she read the note, something fell out of the envelope and onto the floor by her feet.

Tara picked it up and took a closer look. It was an oval-shaped plastic pouch with a picture of a heart inside. Encircling the heart was a crown of thorns, and the thorns had punctured the heart, making it bleed.

"What *is* this?" she asked. "And what's the hole in the top of the pouch for?"

"Oh that's a seal type of thing," Gramma said. "You can put a safety pin through the hole and then pin it to your nighty or to the inside of your housecoat. At least that's what I do. Or you can pin in to your bedsheet near your head so you can see it when you go to sleep and see it again right away in the morning when you wake up."

Why would I want to look at a bleeding heart wearing a crown of thorns every morning? Tara thought. "That's sort of curious, Gramma. Can I have it to pin to my bed at home?"

"Of course you can have that, dear," Gramma said. "You don't mind, do you Mama?"

"Not a'tall. You take it, Tara." Nana nodded, still reading her note.

"So, anyway," Gramma said. "What were you up to this summer before you came here, Tara? Did you go to summer camp?"

"Yup. I was at camp the last two weeks of July and it was so much fun! I was in a cabin called Orion and I made lots of friends. I swam every day and did archery and learned how to canoe and I did all kinds of arts and crafts. I'm happy to be here with you, but I miss being there, too."

"Do you want to go again next year?" Gramma asked, taking a sip of her tea.

"Oh, yes. I want to go every year, and then maybe someday I'll be a counsellor. That's my dream."

"And what else did you do before you got here?" Gramma asked, looking to see if Nana was listening.

"I spent a lot of time visiting my Dad at his barn when Mom was at work," Tara answered, getting off the floor and taking a seat on the couch.

"Who's that, Tara?" Nana asked, as she stopped rocking her chair. "Who is your dad?"

Tara looked back and forth between Nana and Gramma. *Doesn't Nana realize that I have a real dad and a stepdad?*

"Mama, you know that Cathy's first husband is Tara's father, but she's being brought up by Terry, her *step* father. The man Cathy's married to now," Gramma explained.

"So, whose barn do you go to, my dear?" asked Nana.

"Um…well, Terry, I guess, but I call him Dad." Tara shifted on the couch.

Nana opened her eyes wide and started rocking again.

"Don't worry about Mama, dear." Gramma smiled at Tara. "She gets confused about who's who, sometimes."

"Well, anyway, I love being at the barn. When my dad is busy refinishing furniture in the shop, I get to do whatever I want. Did you know that I have a goat named, Bruce?" Tara asked.

Nana and Gramma both shook their heads.

"Yup! He's white with black spots, and he has the cutest pointy horns. You have to be careful though, because as soon as you turn around he tries to butt you in the bum!"

Gramma laughed and Nana just kept rocking, staring wide-eyed at Tara.

"When I'm at the barn," Tara continued. "I find all kinds of animals. I even found a half-dead duck one time. So I picked him up and held him in my arms all day long. Eventually, Dad told me that it was dead, but I thought if I held him long enough, he'd come back to life again."

"You could have made soup out of him, Tara," Nana suggested.

"Mama, no," said Gramma. "That was her pet!"

"Well, he wasn't really my pet," said Tara. "I *did* have a dog though, and his name was Bo. He was a golden retriever, but he got hit by a train one day."

"That's the same as Daddy. He got hit by a train, too," said Gramma.

"God love him and save him," Nana said, crossing herself.

Tara waited until Gramma too had crossed herself before she went on with her story. "And the best thing to do at the barn is swing on the rope up in the hay loft," she said.

"My Lord! What do you mean, swing on a rope?" Gramma asked.

"Well, there are a few older kids who live in the farmhouse not far from the barn. Dad rents the barn from their family, so the kids are still allowed to play in the hay loft," Tara said. "The kids took a great big blue rope and hung it from the centre beam of the barn. There are these small wooden ladders that you can climb up to the platform above the floor, and if someone hands you the rope, you can put your feet or your bum on the big knot at the end and swing back and forth. After you're done swinging, you can just let go of the rope and jump down to the floor."

"My God, Tara, that sounds dangerous!" said Gramma.

Tara just shrugged and went on with her story. "This one time none of the kids were using the rope, so I guess they had just sort of dragged the rope off to the side. It was still attached to the beam, but because it was off to the side you couldn't really swing on it. I wanted to swing, so I climbed the short ladder to the first platform then I made my way over to the next ladder to get up to the second platform. You have to be very careful, though, because the rungs on the ladder turn, and some of them are so loose they actually spin."

Nana and Gramma both stared at Tara, their eyebrows all the way up to their hairlines.

"So up I went, up the second ladder and then the third, until finally I got to the very top of the barn where the beam was. I swung my legs up and over the beam until I was sitting on top. I grabbed the rope, but it was very heavy and hard to slide over the wood. So I pushed and pushed until it started moving toward the centre. I shimmied and pushed, shimmied and pushed, until I made it, with the rope, to the middle of the beam. But once I got there I realized I had to turn around to get back. I looked down and I was up high. I mean really high. But I carefully turned around and started shimmying my way back to the ladder, then down two more ladders and onto the floor again. I looked up and saw that the rope was perfectly positioned for me to swing as much as I wanted." Tara finished her story proudly.

Nana and Gramma blinked and shook their heads.

"Tara. That was a very dangerous thing to do, my dear. You could have killed yourself," Nana said.

"That's what Dad said when he found out what I did. But I didn't know that I wasn't allowed to put the rope back in the middle. I just wanted to move it, so I did," said Tara.

That evening, when it was time to go to bed, Nana told Tara to shut the door to the bedroom.

"Are you alright, Nana? Why do you want the door shut?" Tara asked.

"You get in under the bedclothes now before you catch your death," Nana said quietly. "I have to whisper so Joe can't hear us talking."

"Big Joe? He can't hear us talking, Nana. He's fast asleep in his room at the other side of the house."

Nana squinted at Tara in the semi-dark. "Don't you know that that man can hear the grass growing?"

Tara had no idea what Nana was talking about. Hear the grass growing? Tara had a vision of Big Joe on his hands and knees out in the garden, his ear pressed to the ground, listening to the grass grow. She smiled just thinking of it.

"It's not funny, my dear. It's true," whispered Nana. "Anyway, I wanted to tell you that Rita wants me to give him money for taking me up to the doctor's office. Can you believe that? He's a miser, I tell you. All he wants me here for is to get my money."

"Oh, Nana. That's not why Big Joe wants you here," Tara whispered back. "He's helping Gramma take care of you."

"I don't need anyone to take care of me, my dear," said Nana. "I'm perfectly capable of taking care of myself, except that I need help washing my hair, and my clothes, and making my meals, and that sort of thing. Anyway, like I said, Big Joe's a miser. Now, let's say our prayers and hope to God that he doesn't try to steal my money while we're asleep… O my God, at the end of this day I thank You…"

CHAPTER THIRTEEN

Summer 1982—Last Days at Gramma's

The next morning Tara woke up snuggled behind Nana's back.

She thought about what Nana had said about Big Joe last night. Was Big Joe really out to get Nana's money? From what Tara could tell, Nana didn't have any, and Big Joe had a good job at St. Mary's Cement so why would he need her money? Tara decided that Nana was just being silly and that she had nothing to worry about.

"Are you awake, my dear?" Nana asked quietly from her side of the bed. "If you are, why don't you go over to my dresser there and see what's in the drawer."

Tara loved that dresser. It was the one with three mirrors attached to the top, and all three of them moved on hinges so you could look at yourself from different angles. Tara often pretended she was a famous movie star putting on makeup and doing her hair in those mirrors. Of course, Nana's left-hand drawer was full of powder and rouge, along with her compact and jar of Vaseline. Nana didn't just use Vaseline to straighten her hair and soothe her scalp, she also used it as a salve for her sore finger joints or for any scratch or scrape she might get. Tara had even once seen her take a dollop of the greasy stuff and put it up her nose when she thought it was too dry inside the house.

"Open the drawer on the right and see what's what," Nana said, sitting up and swinging her legs over the side of the bed.

Tara opened the drawer and took out a set of rosary beads, a picture of the Virgin Mary, and a prayer book from The Sisters of the Precious Blood. At the very bottom of the drawer, on top of a pile of tissues, there was a small handful of Tara's favourite: Scotch mints.

"I love these, Nana, thank you," she said as she popped one into her mouth.

"Well, you can come in here and take a few any time you want, but don't tell anyone they're there or they'll be gone in an instant," Nana whispered.

Downstairs, Gramma was sitting at the kitchen table, listening to the news and smoking a cigarette. She often doodled on her tablet when she was at the table, and today Tara saw that she'd drawn her famous cup and saucer picture and several of her smiling cat pictures. When Tara walked in, Gramma gave her a big smile.

"You look excited about something, Gramma."

"Well, did I tell you that my sister Katie is coming for a visit today? She lives in Brantford and she wants to come over to see Mama."

Tara knew all about Aunt Kay and where she lived, but she guessed that Gramma had forgotten that she'd already told Tara—many times before—about Aunt Kay.

"I think it will be good for Katie to come for a visit and get out of Brantford for a while," said Gramma. "She seems a little depressed if you ask me. Here, listen to this letter she wrote back around Christmas time." She shuffled through a pile of letters that she kept beside the radio.

"Hi Rita, how are you? I hope you are fine and looking forward to Xmas. I'm not. I couldn't care less. Maybe the boys will be around for Xmas. My left hip and back is paining like hell because it's so damp today. I wish it was summer. Ha ha.

"How are Doug and Elsie? Joanie, do you see her? Or Rosie? It's so queer Mickey in BC, you, Joanie and Doug in Stratford, my Kimmie in Halifax, Rosie in Mount Forest, and me in Brantford. We are all over the place.

"Write when you can. I love getting letters but hate writing them. Why don't you come down for a weekend? Before we kick the bucket. Ha ha. I think I will lay down for a bit. I don't feel very well. Love, your sister, Katie."

"What does she mean by 'kick the bucket'?" Tara asked. "Does she mean you might die?"

"Oh, she's just kidding. She has a quite a sense of humour, but she's right. I should go down to Brantford sometime and see her. But for now I can't leave Mama, so I'm glad Katie's coming here."

Aunt Kay arrived later that afternoon, and Tara was excited to see her again. Her son dropped her off, but he couldn't come in because he had to get back to work. "See ya, Ma. I'll pick you up in a few hours," he said as he headed down the porch stairs. "'Bye ladies." He waved goodbye over his head.

"Hi, Katie. How are you?" Gramma asked as she took Aunt Kay's purse and put it on the bench.

"Hey, Reet! You look good, how are you feeling?" Aunt Kay took her purse back and pulled out a pack of cigarettes. "Where's Mama?"

"Hi, Aunt Kay. Remember me?" Tara said with a smile.

"Of course I do, Tara! How could I forget? Anyway, how's tricks?" She put her arms around Tara and gave her a big hug.

Tara was surprised at how strong she was. She was such a tiny person. She looked a lot like Gramma, but a bit smaller and skinnier. She had the same short, curly dark hair with grey running through it, but she wore a bit more makeup than Gramma—more rouge and lipstick, and her eyebrows were pencilled in. She was dressed in a white cotton blouse with the shortest pair of jean shorts Tara had ever seen on a woman her age. But she moved as if she were a lot younger than Gramma. She was "spry," as they say.

Aunt Kay walked quickly into the kitchen and then into the living room. "Where's Mama?" she asked again.

"She's been having a nap up in her room since lunch. She'll wake up in a while," answered Gramma

"Well, since she's sleeping, I'm starting to feel a tad thirsty."

"Do you want a hot tea, Katie?"

"Hell, no, I need a cold beer!" She went out to the front porch and came back with a full case of Labatt Blue. "Will this be enough for us, do ya think?" She winked at her sister.

Aunt Kay had a way of pushing out her lower jaw when she talked and inhaling sharply every time she said the word "Yup!"

"It's kind of early, isn't it?" Gramma asked as she looked around, almost as if to see who would know if she drank a beer in the middle of the day.

"There's no time like the present!" Aunt Kay ripped open the case, grabbed two beers, and handed one to her sister. "Do ya have a bottle opener handy?"

Tara knew exactly where it was and ran to get it for her great-aunt and her grandmother. The three of them sat out on the porch and talked and talked. Tara always thought that Gramma talked a lot, but she had nothing on Aunt Kay. Aunt Kay talked very fast, and she had a thicker Cape Breton accent than Gramma. She also had this way of pressing her teeth together when she inhaled, so when she took a breath it sounded almost like a hiss. Tara thought this was hilarious, and could listen to her talk all day.

Aunt Kay had her feet up on her case of Blue and kept crossing and recrossing her legs, admiring how they looked in those short-shorts of hers. The sisters were talking about Brantford in the 1940s, when they'd lived at the Women's Residence while working at the artillery factory.

"Remember when you broke your damned foot, Reet?" Aunt Kay laughed as she exhaled cigarette smoke. "You were sneaking out of the dormitory, heading out to meet some guy at the dance."

"Oh my God, Katie. I was climbing out the window and I lost my balance and fell right to the ground. My foot didn't hurt at first, so I went out and danced on it all night!"

"Yup!" Aunt Kay inhaled. "And by the time you got home, your foot was black and blue," she hissed, her jaw working in and out.

"It was never right again after that. I should have gone to the doctor," Gramma said.

"Yeah, right, and then the floor mother would have known you snuck out for sure," Aunt Kay snorted.

"Well, with all the pain I still have with that foot, maybe I should have been more careful."

"But Reet, it was worth it, wasn't it? Those were the days." She clenched her teeth together and exhaled slowly, looking out over the street. "I miss those times…when we were young and single, with no kids or a husband to worry about."

"Well, it's in the past now, Katie. No sense in getting caught up in those memories from long ago." Gramma checked her pack and noticed that she was down to only a few cigarettes.

"Tara, dear, can you run up to the Handy and get me another pack of cigarettes, please?"

Tara was always ready to run up to the Handy for Gramma because there was often money left over to buy candy.

She followed Gramma as she went inside to dial the Handy. "Hello, Lois? It's Rita from 98 Railway. How are you? That's good to hear. Well, I'm alright. My sister Katie is here visiting me. Yes. Oh yes, Mama's fine, she's having a sleep. Thanks for asking about her. Well, listen dear, the reason I'm calling is because I'm sending my granddaughter, Tara, to get a pack of Black Cats for me. I'll give her the money. Yes. Yes. OK, that's grand. Thank you. Bye-bye now."

Gramma fished her change purse out of her apron pocket and handed Tara a rolled up two dollar bill. "Alright, dear, Lois will have the Black Cats ready for you, and then you can spend what's left over."

Looking both ways, Tara crossed the road and walked up another two blocks until she got to Dufferin Street. The Handy was on the same street as the park, and it was actually an old house situated smack-dab where two other streets met so it sort of looked like it was sitting on an island.

Tara pulled open the door and there was Lois, smiling at her from behind the glass counter.

"Well, there you are, Tara. How nice to see you again," Lois said.

"Hi, Lois. Are you having a nice day?" Tara asked. Lois was one of the nicest people Tara had ever met, and she was always excited to see her when she was working.

"Oh, sure, sure. Every day is nice when you work in the Handy." Lois laughed. "Alright now, here's your grandmother's Black Cats and, here, I already have the change ready for you. Now, take a look under the glass and see what tickles your fancy."

By the time Tara got home with her paper bag full of candy the party was over. The half-empty case of Blue had been stowed away under the porch, Aunt Kay was sitting with her knees together and her ankles crossed, and Gramma had put away the ashtray. Nana was sitting in a lawn chair they had set up for her, and they all had tea cups in their hands and were talking quietly about how everyone down home was getting along.

After a while, Aunt Kay looked at her watch. "Well, folks! My ride will be here any minute and I don't want to keep him waiting." She stood up and gathered her things. "Goodbye, Tara. Make sure you tell your mother I said hi next time you see her. You know, she was always my favourite niece. Well, my favourite after Young Rose, but anyway, I love your mom a lot so you make sure you tell her that, OK?"

After Aunt Kay left, Gramma, Tara, and Nana went inside so Gramma could get supper started. That evening, Gramma let Tara have a shower all by herself and Tara was happy that there wasn't any sandbox sand itching her this time.

The next morning, Tara packed her suitcase to be ready for when her mom came to pick her up. She was sad to leave Gramma's after having been there so long. She loved their routine, and she liked how they went around like two peas in a pod, but at the same time she was looking forward to seeing her mother and going back to Kitchener for the rest of the summer.

It was early afternoon when her mom pulled into the driveway. To Tara's surprise, her brother Ronnie had come too. Ronnie was thirteen years old, just a few years younger than Joey. *He must have come back from Alberta, where he'd been since the beginning of July.*

"Hi, Ronnie!" Tara ran over and hugged her brother. "How was Alberta? Did you have fun?"

"Hey, Tara. Alberta was alright, I guess," said Ronnie with a shrug.

"Hi, little girl! I've missed you," her mom said, giving Tara a big hug.

"I missed you too, Mom," Tara said, holding her mom tight.

At that moment, Gramma and Joey came out onto the porch and walked down the steps.

"Hi, Joey. How are you doing?" Tara's mom put her hands on Joey's shoulders. "I've been thinking about you a lot. Let's make sure we talk later about what's going on in your life, OK?"

"Mom, guess what?" Tara interrupted. "Aunt Kay was here for a visit."

"Oh, I would have loved to see her!" Her mom's face lit up. "Isn't she so funny? How is she doing?"

"She told all kinds of funny stories about when her and Gramma were young and living in Brantford," said Tara. "Oh, and she said to say hello to you and that you are her favourite niece. Well, besides Young Rose, she said."

Tara's mom's smile disappeared. She pressed her lips together, shook her head, and walked up the stairs to the porch and straight into the house.

After Gramma hugged Ronnie and asked how his trip had been, she followed her daughter into the house, leaving the kids alone on the walkway.

"Hey, Ronnie," said Joey.

"Hey, Joey. Wanna hang out in the car?" asked Ronnie.

Tara wanted Ronnie to come in the house so she could tell him about her holiday at Gramma's. She wanted to tell him about Ginger and Big Joe and Aunt Kay, and show him where she danced and where the records were, but he and Joey just went and sat in the car. *What were they doing? What were they talking about? Why had they locked the doors?*

"Can I come in and sit with you guys?" she asked through the closed window.

"Why don't you just go in the house," Ronnie said.

"No. I want to hang out with you guys. Let me in," she insisted.

Looking irritated, Joey unlocked the door so she could get in the back seat. She listened to them talk for a while, but they were just talking about boring stuff so she got back out of the car and went and sat on the porch steps, watching them. She quickly got bored of that so she went back to the car, but when she tried opening the back door she found it was locked again.

She knocked on the window. "Hey, you two, let me in."

Joey rolled down the window. "Do you want in or do you want out? Make up your mind."

"I want in." They unlocked the door and again she got in the back seat. "Do you guys want to go in the house and get a drink? Why do you two want to sit in the car? You're so boring!"

"OK, sure. Let's go in the house," said Ronnie. The boys looked at each other and smirked.

They both jumped out of the car and then held the door handle so Tara couldn't open the door. "Let go of the door handle so I can get out," she said.

"Do you want in or do you want out?" Joey asked again.

"I thought you said you wanted to stay in the car. So, why do you want out?" Ronnie laughed.

"Let go of the door handle!" Tara yelled as she tried desperately to open the door from the inside.

"Nope."

They both laughed, watching her freak out in the back seat like a bug caught in a jar.

Tara started screaming. "Let me out, you jerks! Let me OUT!"

Finally, they walked away from the car, and as if they hadn't done anything wrong, walked up the steps and into the house.

Tara hated to be locked in anywhere and she felt like crying, but she was so mad she'd rather hit them both in the head than cry. Sweating and shaking, she jumped out of the car and ran into the house.

"Mom! Ronnie and Joey are such jerks! They locked me in the car and wouldn't let me out!"

Her mom was sitting in the living room beside Nana, and Gramma was in the kitchen doing the dishes.

"Tara, calm down, you're shaking like a leaf." She shot a look at Ronnie, who was sitting on the back couch eating those weird candies from the wooden walnut. "Ronnie, what the heck is going on?"

"She's freaking out for no reason, Mom. We were just playing," he said as he popped a dust-covered candy into his mouth.

"They were not," Tara yelled. "They were being mean to me and I hate them!"

Gramma came into the living room, shaking two pills out of the ASA bottle. "Tara. Don't say that, dear, you don't hate your brother and your uncle."

"Well, maybe I do. Ronnie is a jerk and Joey is a lazy, spoiled brat! He always changes the channel when we're watching something, he sleeps in all day, and he can't even help you with the vacuuming on account of his fake allergies!"

Suddenly, Gramma shot across the room and grabbed Tara's arm and squeezed it hard. "Don't you ever say that about my Joey again. Who do you think you are, saying something nasty like that?" Gramma's face was pale and she was shaking.

Tara was shocked. Gramma had never talked to her like that before, and she had certainly never grabbed her like that before either. Tara's throat tightened and tears started welling up. For the first time in her life, she realized that maybe Gramma loved someone more than her and that broke her heart a little bit.

"Maybe you should go sit by yourself somewhere and think about how sorry you are that you said such a mean thing about my son!" Gramma roughly let go of Tara's arm.

Tara ran through the front hall and sat on the stairs underneath the African Violets, silent tears streaming down her face.

"Mom," she heard her mom say. "Don't you think that was a bit harsh? The boys must have really scared Tara for her to react like that."

"I can't let anyone talk about my son like that, Cathy," Gramma said in a strong voice.

"Oh, I see. Well, you certainly have a lot of gumption when you want to stick up for your precious son. Too bad you never had that when you should have been sticking up for me all those years."

"Cathy, what are you talking about? I've always stuck up for you," said Gramma.

"Ha! That's a good one, Mom. You let Mrs. Wrenn treat me like a second-class citizen for years. You never stuck up for me, not once."

Tara imagined that her mom was looking around for a way to escape, and then she heard her say, "C'mon Ronnie, get in the car."

"Cathy!"

"No, Mom. I'm leaving. I'm not going to do this again." Tara heard her mom's voice grow louder as she came into the front hall.

"Where's my purse?" She looked around and snatched it from the bench where she'd left it. "Tara! Let's go."

"Cathy, my dear, don't leave." Tara could hear Nana calling from her rocking chair in the living room.

"Sorry, Nana." Tara's mom walked back to the living room and kissed Nana quickly on the cheek. "I have to get out of here." As she went back through the front hall, she said, "Tara, get off those steps and get in the car."

And, once again, the car peeled out of the driveway and no one talked all the way home.

———— •〜〜• ————

It was a few days after they'd left Stratford that Gramma called Tara to apologize.

"I'm so sorry, dear, that I squeezed your arm. I just love my Joey so much, and what you said about him really hurt my feelings," said Gramma.

"I know, Gramma, and I'm sorry too. I don't actually think Joey is lazy. I was just scared being locked in the car, and I was real mad at Ronnie and Joey."

"Well, I really am sorry that I got upset with you," said Gramma. "You know how much I love you, right?"

"Yes, and I love you too, Gramma."

After Tara hung up the phone, she told her mom that Gramma had called to apologize.

"She apologized to you?" Her mom shook her head while she sprayed Windex on the kitchen window. "Well, that was easy, wasn't it?"

Tara thought her mom would be happy that Gramma said she was sorry. "I guess so," she said. "I didn't like having Gramma mad at me, so I'm glad we're back to normal."

"It must be nice for the two of you to have a quick chat and then everything is suddenly fine." Her mom pressed her lips together and went back to cleaning.

"Mom, are you mad at me?" Tara didn't know why this conversation was making her mom mad, and she was starting to feel a bit confused.

Her mom sighed, threw the paper towel into the garbage, and sat down on one of the dining room chairs.

"No, little girl, I'm not mad at you. But sometimes I feel like…oh, I can't say how I feel, it's so childish."

"Tell me, Mom, it's OK."

"Well, I kind of feel like…why couldn't I have been more like you? When you tell me about going to Stratford and spending time with Mom and Big Joe and Nana, I feel jealous. Isn't that ridiculous? I mean, Mom never listened to records or watched TV with me, and she didn't play cards with me or give me money to go to the store. She certainly didn't bathe me and wash my hair, and when you tell me she did all that with you it makes me feel like bawling."

Tara didn't know what to say, so she put her arms around her mother and hugged her.

"For God's sake, I'm acting like a baby, aren't I," her mom said.

"No, Mom, you're upset and it's OK if you want to tell me how you feel." Tara sat on the other dining room chair.

"And when you tell me that Big Joe buys you your favourite foods and lets you put rollers in his hair, I just can't get over that," her mom said, continuing her story. "He hardly ever even spoke to me when I was a kid—unless he was yelling. And, also, you get to sleep with Nana. Do you know how many nights I dreamed of sleeping in Nana's bed with her? But I always had to fight for her attention, and most times I lost out because there was always someone else who needed more attention than me. Nana said that I was calm, cool, and collected, so maybe she thought I didn't need a hug or affection or anything that made me feel like she loved me, but I did, and I desperately wanted it from her because I loved her so much." She reached for a tissue and dabbed at her eyes.

"Mom, I'm pretty sure Nana loves you. I mean, look at all the things you do for her, all the running around you do and how often you go to visit her. And Gramma loves you too, you know. I mean, she must love you more than me. I think that people love their children the most, and then their grandchildren after that, so you don't have to worry about Gramma loving me more than you." Tara's throat tightened and her eyes pricked with tears.

"Oh, honey, that's not what I want you to think." Her mom took her hand and squeezed it. "Me and all my issues have nothing to do with you. I'm happy that you have a relationship with Gramma, and I wouldn't deny you that for the world. I just can't believe that she tells you that she loves you. I don't remember her ever telling me that she loved me."

Tara saw more tears welling up in her mother's eyes.

"I shouldn't be sharing these childish feelings with you, and I don't want you to feel bad at all. I love you so much, and I want you to be loved by everyone else too. Just ignore me." She blew her nose and smiled weakly at Tara, then pulled her into her arms and held her tight.

"I love you, little girl, don't ever forget that."

CHAPTER FOURTEEN

Summer 1983—Avon Crest

It was August, and Tara's summer visit had been postponed again.

Last winter, between Christmas and New Year's Eve, Nana had had several more serious nose bleeds and had been in and out of the hospital because as soon as they would cauterize one nostril, the other one would bleed. They had given her all kinds of medication, but nothing had worked. She would get nosebleed after nosebleed, and Gramma had been beside herself trying to take care of her.

One winter evening, when Gramma had been heading up to the hospital to visit Nana, she'd fallen on a sheet of ice and broke her other hip in several places. Gramma said they'd rushed her in for X-rays, but had ended up leaving her in a room with no pain medication until two o'clock the next day. She had said, "If there was a hell, I was surely living in it when they forgot about me in that room. I will never forget that pain as long as I live."

Then, in early spring, Nana had what they called a gastric ulcer, and Gramma had said that when Nana took the medication she'd get dizzy and weak and couldn't get out of bed. She'd then started taking all kinds of laxatives because her bowels wouldn't move, but then she couldn't pass any urine and ended up with a bad urinary tract infection. Nana had been in the hospital for two weeks because of it, and had been unable to get back to Gramma's and settled enough to enjoy her eightieth birthday celebration.

But now that it was August and everyone seemed healthy and happy, Tara was finally allowed to go to Stratford for her summer visit. This time, her mom said that since she was nine years old now, she was grown-up enough to take the train from Kitchener to Stratford. Tara was a little nervous, but mostly excited to ride the train. Her mom brought her into the station, bought her a ticket, and then waited with her until the train pulled in.

"Now, don't forget to keep your ticket out because the conductor will come by and want to see it. If you don't have a ticket, they'll stop the train and kick you off and then you'll have to walk all the way to Stratford."

Tara knew her mom was just kidding, but she made sure to have her ticket ready anyway.

The ride only took thirty minutes, but it was so smooth and Tara was so preoccupied with the scenes rushing by outside her window that it only felt like a few minutes. Big Joe was waiting for her on the platform when she arrived in Stratford. He didn't say much, but he smiled and took her bag. The drive to 98 Railway was very slow and very quiet. Big Joe was a man of few words, but Tara was comfortable with the silence.

When they arrived at the house, Tara ran in, kicl

shoes, and went looking for Gramma. As soon as Ta

the kitchen, she noticed that the room seemed bright

"Hi Tara! What do you think?" Gramma asked, §

a hug. "Big Joe and Joey did some painting over the v

it nice when the baseboards, window sills, and door ca

a fresh coat of white paint? What a difference it mak

Tara looked around and thought everything

cleaner than usual. They'd all been here at Christmas,

time the house was its usual dusty and comfortable s

looked like the carpets had been vacuumed, the f

shiny, and the shelves and the cupboards were free

looked really nice, but Tara thought it was odd for tl

be so clean.

"Did you get a cleaning lady or something, Gra

asked.

"No, dear, but you know what? All last winter m

paining and my sinuses were really bothering me. I l

Sinutab with codeine twice a day, but they weren't wor

doctor ordered a brain scan and he said that my he

much because of my back pain," Gramma explained

thought I would just have to live with it, but then the d

me back and said he'd figured it all had to do with m

Tara had to admit that Gramma's teeth, althoug!

somewhat straight, had always been mostly brown in

a few of them had fallen out.

"The doctor made me an appointment, and §

They took out every single last one of my teeth ai

em with these." She smiled wide at Tara, showing off all her
ew white teeth. "How do ya like them apples?"

"Gramma, they look so good! So, does your head feel better
ow?" asked Tara, admiring Gramma's new smile.

"Oh, yes, it's like a miracle, really. I feel so much better, and
think I have more energy so I've been cleaning as much as I
n, while I can. If I could only get rid of the pain in my hips,
y feet, my back, and my legs, I'd be right as rain." She laughed.

"Well, I'm glad that the new teeth helped a little, at least."
ara smiled. "Where's Nana? I can't wait to see her."

"She's sleeping right now, dear. She hasn't been feeling well
all, and I'm starting to get worried." Gramma's smile faded.

"I thought she was better now since she's been home from
e hospital."

"She was doing alright for a while there, but she's sleeping
 the time and she just seems so weak," said Gramma. "I've
en praying for her every day."

The next day, Nana didn't come down at nine o'clock for
eakfast like she normally did, so Gramma went up to see how
e was doing. When she came back down the stairs, her face
is pale and she was shaking like a leaf.

"I have to call the hospital, dear. Something's wrong with
ama," Gramma whispered, barely able to find her voice.

The ambulance came right away and took Nana to the hospital.
g Joe took Gramma up to see her, but he came back right away
stay with Tara while they waited to see what was happening. In
 meantime, Big Joe called Tara's mom in Kitchener to let her
ow that Nana had been rushed to the hospital.

When Tara's mom arrived in Stratford a half hour later, she too told Tara to stay put while she went up to the hospital to see what was going on with Nana. Eventually, her mom came back to the house with Gramma and told Tara that they had to head back to Kitchener. On the way home, her mom explained that Nana was very sick. She was having trouble with her bowels—they had ruptured—and there was poison all through her body. The doctors had operated and got it all under control, but they had to keep Nana at the hospital and monitor her for at least a few weeks.

Once Tara got back home, she felt a little lost. She hadn't wanted to leave Gramma's house, but she understood that Gramma was upset and nervous about Nana and would want to be available to see her whenever she could and be ready as soon as Nana could come home. Little did anyone know, Nana would not be going back to Gramma's ever again.

———————•⟨∞⟩•———————

The rest of the month made for a gruelling routine. Tara and her mom got up early every morning, ate a quick breakfast, and then got in the car to head to Stratford. They would stop by Gramma's house to say hello and see if she wanted a ride up to see Nana. Then, whether Gramma went with them or not, they would head across town to visit Nana. They would usually stay all day, stop at Aunt Joanie's on the way home for a visit and a tea, and then eventually head back to Kitchener. The next day, they would do it all over again.

Tara's mom said the doctors had been hoping that Nana would come around, but apparently she was getting worse. Her mom explained that Nana now had a colostomy bag, but couldn't seem to gain her strength back. She couldn't keep food or liquids down, she vomited almost every day, and she was in a lot of pain. By now, the staff at Stratford General Hospital had moved Nana to a palliative care facility across the street. It was called Avon Crest.

When Tara's mom had taken her to visit Nana in the hospital, Tara realized she really didn't like hospitals. She didn't like the smell, she didn't like how sick the people looked, and she didn't like the idea that it was possible that people could die. But, the palliative care place, Avon Crest, was much worse. Tara knew that the people there were very sick—terminal, her mom called it. The building itself looked like it was falling apart. It was made of darkened yellow brick, and what had been painted white was now worn and chipped. The front facade of Avon Crest had endless rows of dark windows, and the roof was littered with pointed gables and turrets and broken chimneys. Even when the weather was nice, Avon Crest always seemed to be dreary, as if it lived endlessly under a dark cloud. To Tara, it looked like an insane asylum from the scary movies she watched with her friends.

Tara couldn't believe that poor Nana had to stay at Avon Crest, and even though Tara loved Nana and wanted to visit her, she always got the creeps when her and her mom walked through the big doors of the old building.

"C'mon, Tara, I know you don't like this place, but we have to hurry up before the lunchtime service starts," Tara's mom said as they made their way up one flight of stairs and then down the hallway to Nana's room.

They crept in so they didn't disturb Nana, who looked like she was finally resting. Tara knew Nana didn't like hospitals and didn't trust the nurses, so it was hard for her to get a good sleep or feel like she was being taken care of properly. Nana didn't trust the pills or the medications, or what was in the IV, and she especially didn't trust the lady who was sharing her room with her.

As soon as Tara and her mom got close to the bed, Nana slowly opened her big brown eyes. "Aww, Cathy, for the love of God, you're here. And, Tara, is that you, my dear? God love you for coming to see me here in this hell hole."

"Nana, it's alright now. Close your eyes and go back to sleep. We'll stay here until you wake up," said her mom.

"Oh no, dear, I can't go back to sleep," said Nana. "If I go back to sleep, that lady over there will kill me."

"What? Nana, what are you talking about?" asked Tara's mom. "She looks like a nice old lady. She looks like she's sleeping quite peacefully."

"You think she looks peaceful? Well, my dear, you've got another thing coming," Nana whispered. "She keeps a pair of scissors in her gown pocket, and the other night, while everyone else was sleeping and the nurses were having their break, she whispered to me that as soon as I went to sleep she was going to come over here and stab me to death."

Tara and her mom looked over at the woman to make sure she was still sleeping. Putting her hand on Tara's shoulder to signal her to stay back, her mom tiptoed across the room and leaned in close to look around the lady's bed. Suddenly, she stood up straight and turned to look at Tara and Nana. Her eyes were wide and her eyebrows had shot up to her hairline. She pointed at the food tray that was still on the table beside the lady's bed, then picked up what she'd found—a pair of scissors!

She quickly made her way back to Nana's bed. "For God almighty sake, Nana," she whispered. "You're right!"

"Didn't I tell you, dear? She wants to stab me while I'm sleeping."

Tara's mom went to the nursing station and told the nurses what she'd found. When she got back, she told Tara and Nana that the nurses said they were glad she'd brought the scissors to them because it had been reported that one of the nurses had misplaced her pair. The nurses admitted that the lady was suffering from something called ICU psychosis, and that she was delirious and paranoid and possibly a little dangerous. The doctors had said to use straps to keep her arms bound to her bed, but apparently someone had forgotten to tie them.

"Oh my God, Nana, you could have been seriously hurt," said her mom. "I'm going to get that woman moved out of this room as soon as possible."

Soon after, a nurse came into the room and rolled the lady and her things out into the hallway. "Don't worry, we'll find a private room for this one, and your grandmother will be fine now and able to rest," said the nurse.

Once Nana got settled and comfortable, and they'd assured her that she would be safe, they promised to come back after Nana had had her lunch.

"Are you hungry, little girl?" Tara's mom asked as they walked out of the room.

"Yes, I'm starving. Can we go to McDonald's on the way home?"

"Oh, we're not going home yet," said her mom. "We'll have our lunch and then go back again to stay with Nana until the rest of them come to visit this afternoon."

Tara had been hoping they could go back home, or maybe go to Gramma's house, but she understood that nothing was more important right now than making sure Nana was safe and sound.

"We'll just go to the hospital cafeteria across the street to get soup and a sandwich and a hot tea. By then, Nana should be finished her lunch and then we can get back to our visit."

Oh God, Tara thought. Most people would think that going to the hospital cafeteria meant getting the heck out of this place, going out into the sunshine, and crossing the street to a nice, bright hospital cafeteria. But no, this lovely place had what most people have nightmares about: an underground tunnel. The tunnel went from Avon Crest to the hospital's basement, and Tara knew what was in hospital basements—bodies, probably dead ones.

Through a set of metal doors at the end of the hallway, Tara followed her mom down two flights of stairs—down, down, down—until they reached another thick metal door. Tara's mom swung it open and the stale breeze that came from the underground tunnel blew stray hairs away from their faces.

"What sort of germy particles do you think are flying around in this breeze, Mom?" Tara asked with a shudder.

"Oh, Tara, it's just a tunnel," her mom said. "It's nothing to be afraid of."

"Mom, it's an *underground* tunnel, and I can't believe we're going through it."

Going on for what seemed like miles, the tunnel was painted a sickly hospital green. The ceiling lights only illuminated the floor directly below, creating dark spaces between the circles of light. All along the tunnel walls was door after door—all closed, all securely locked. *What's behind those doors?* Tara didn't want to know. She fought back an overwhelming need to run because she knew that running would only awaken what was sure to be lurking in those dark spaces. She took her mother's hand, faced forward, and started walking as quickly as she could toward the safety of the hospital basement. *Pretty sad state of affairs*, she thought, to think that the hospital basement was going to be the safe haven.

"It's just a convenient way for the nurses and the doctors to go back and forth between the hospital and Avon Crest without having to go outside and around to the front doors," her mother said, taking longer strides to keep up.

"Are you kidding me, Mom? I'm pretty sure this is where they keep dead bodies, and God only knows what else. This has got to be the creepiest place I've ever been in."

Suddenly, Tara got the heebie jeebies so bad she let go of her mom's hand and ran toward the big metal doors at the end of the tunnel. She pushed them open, and only when her mom was safely beside her and the doors were shut did she feel safe from the terrors of the tunnel.

"My goodness, Tara, you have quite an imagination! There are no dead bodies down here."

"Well, where do you think they keep them then, Mom?"

Her mom thought about it for a second. "Eww, maybe you're right. Let's get the heck upstairs!"

They ate their lunch in the warm stream of sunlight that came in the window of the first-floor cafeteria. Tara wished she was out in that sun, playing at the park or sitting on Gramma's porch.

"What time can we go home, Mom? I'd like to call on my friends and play outside for a while"

"Let's just go visit Nana for a bit and then we'll head home, OK?"

"OK, but if we have to go back to Avon Crest, can I ask a favour? Can we please leave here by the front door and not back through that wretched tunnel?"

After, when they had visited with Nana for about an hour, there was a sudden commotion in the hallway outside her room. Tara looked up to see a small group of women she recognized. Gramma, Marlene, Joanie, Big Molly, and Janey had arrived for their visit. Tara was happy that Big Molly and Janey were able to fly up to Ontario so quickly.

Tara jumped up from where she sat at the end of Nana's bed and ran over to Gramma. "Hi, Gramma! How are you?"

"Oh, dear, well it's been a hard couple days. But I've been missing you," Gramma said with sad eyes and a weak smile.

Tara gave her a gentle hug and kissed her on the cheek. She went around and hugged all the women, and then stood beside her Aunt Marlene while everyone else gathered around Nana's bed. The women went around refilling the water jug, checking the colostomy bag, plumping up Nana's pillows, checking to see if she'd taken her pills, and patted her hands and kissed her cheeks. Tara felt bad for them. She knew how much each and every one of them loved Nana. Nana had a special place in their hearts, and it made Tara happy—but it also made her want to cry—to see the love shared between them all.

"Can I get you a cup of tea, Mama?" Gramma asked Nana, looking around to see where she could get some tea from.

"No, Mom, she's only supposed to have water. The nurse said that a million times," Tara's mom said impatiently. "Just sit there and relax while we take care of Nana."

Gramma's face dropped a little, but she went over to the chair near the window and sat down. Tara knew Gramma didn't like feeling useless, and she worried when Gramma started shuffling through her purse looking for her ASAs.

Aunt Marlene put her arm around Tara's shoulder and said, "Tara, would you like to come with me down to the waiting room? I saw that there's a vending machine down there, and guess what? It's full of chocolate bars and little bags of cookies."

Tara could always count on Aunt Marlene for the comfort of food, especially the kind of food made of sugar and calories.

After a few more hours, and once everyone felt satisfied that Nana was settled for the evening, they all decided to go back to Aunt Joanie's for their much-needed cups of hot tea. Tara had wanted to go home, but now that she was with her family she didn't want to be anywhere else. She felt lucky to be surrounded by so many kind and caring women, and was content to sit and listen to them talk about what was going on, what they should do, and what would happen to Nana. Tara made sure to sit by Gramma and pay attention to her when she wanted to give her opinion or share her ideas.

Finally, a long time after the sun had set, Cathy turned to Tara and said, "Well, little girl, I think it's time we get you home and in bed. Tomorrow will be another long day and you need your sleep."

And so went the days for another two weeks. Back and forth between Kitchener and Stratford, between Avon Crest and the hospital cafeteria, between Joanie's house and Gramma's house. Tara got caught up in the routine of it all and thought that, any day, Nana would get better and finally be able to leave that horrible place.

And she did leave that place, but not because she got better.

CHAPTER FIFTEEN

November 1983—Conversations About the Past

By the beginning of September, the decision had been made.

Nana knew she wasn't getting better, and if she only had a bit of time left she wanted to spend it down home in Cape Breton. Tara didn't want to understand what this meant. She wanted Nana to go back to Gramma's so they could play cards, listen to records, and say their prayers. She didn't want Nana to leave, and wished she didn't understand what they meant by only a "bit of time."

Tara blinked and stared at her mom. "Is she really not getting better, Mom?" She choked back a sob.

"Tara, this isn't what we were hoping for, but I have to be honest with you," her mom explained, holding her hand, "Nana is dying and she wants to go home."

They were sitting in their house at the kitchen table. "The doctors are saying that she only has a few months to live. She had the ruptured bowel, but now they've found that she also has cancer and it's so far gone that they can't do anything for her."

Tara's mom closed her eyes and covered her face with her hands. After a moment, she let out a ragged sob, then reached out and pulled Tara close. Tara buried her face into her mom's neck and let her own tears stream down her cheeks. After a while, Tara grabbed a Kleenex and handed it to her mom. Her mom wiped her eyes and blew her nose and said, "So, anyway, since Big Molly and Janey have already left, it's up to me and Marlene to take Nana home."

Tara couldn't imagine how Nana would manage a flight all the way to Cape Breton. She was so weak and tired and she had the colostomy bag, and even though she took all kinds of pain pills Tara knew she still felt a lot of pain in her side where the incision had been made.

"While we're gone I'm going to send you to Gramma's, OK? She'd love to have you, and the two of you get along so well it'll be best to have you stay with her."

———————•⟨∽⟩•———————

The week she spent with Gramma wasn't at all like it normally was. All the kids had gone back to school so the park was empty, and there was a chill in the air so it wasn't comfortable sitting on the porch. Gramma had a lot of pain in her ankle so they couldn't walk uptown or go to the library, and she had a bad cold so she didn't have the energy to sing and dance with Tara in the kitchen.

Big Joe went to work every day, and seemed more grouchy than usual when he got home. He still left cookies for Tara in his lunch box, but for the most part he'd just come home, eat, and lay on his couch. Joey was in and out of the house going to school, out with his friends, or to work at the restaurant. He would come home from work late at night and want to unwind and watch TV, so he would tell Gramma that Tara would have go sleep upstairs in his room instead of on the couch. He would then sleep on her couch, instead. Tara hadn't liked that idea, but she didn't want to argue and make Gramma upset.

It rained most of the time, and the house was dreary and quiet. She and Gramma watched soap operas all day, and late in the afternoon Gramma would ask Tara to do the dishes or the vacuuming so that she could make a simple supper for the three of them. Gramma didn't want to play cards or draw on brown paper bags, she just wanted to sit in her chair, smoke cigarettes, and write in her diary. Every few hours she would make her way into the kitchen and go through the cupboard to get either Motrin, ASAs, or Sinutab. She'd make tea and once or twice Tara noticed that Gramma reached behind Big Joe's couch to grab the bottle of light-brown stuff. Tara was worried about Gramma. She knew Gramma was sick with worry about Nana, and hated the idea that she was so far away. But to Tara, her grandmother seemed more than just sad.

One day, while Gramma was in the basement putting the wet laundry in the dryer, Tara quietly went over to the table beside the chair and opened her diary. It was dark green and had 1978 stamped on the front. Tara opened it and saw that the diary went all the way from late 1978 to this morning. She flipped to the most recent entry.

My husband is gone to work, my granddaughter is sleeping, and so is my son, but then he'll be off to work too. I wash the dishes, I clean up, I watch TV, I write in my

diary, I read my book, and I make supper, over and over
again. One day leads into the next. I used to always write
that I need to make Mama her breakfast, and Lord, I wish
I could write that now. What I wouldn't give to have her
here with me so we could have a tea and talk like we used
to do.

Sometimes, dear diary, when I think back over the
years, I wonder where all the time has gone and it makes
me feel so sad and lonesome. But I guess the best thing to
do for depression is to wrap up the past, put a pretty blue
ribbon on it, and look at things the way they are now and
let the future take care of itself. A person could easily be
depressed all the time if they let sadness from the past rule
them. I guess a person should take each new day and look
forward to filling it with being kind and considerate of
others. And, as long as you have God on your side,
everything will turn out just fine.

Tara closed the diary and went to sit on the couch. Her
heart ached for Gramma. She wanted to make her feel better,
but she didn't know what to do. A hot cup of tea wasn't going
to be enough this time, so she decided that when Gramma came
back up from the basement she would turn the TV off and just
sit and talk. Gramma loved to talk, and so she would listen.

"Do you want to look at the photo albums, Gramma? I bet
I can rhyme off all the names of your whole family."

At first it seemed like Gramma wanted to turn the TV back
on again, but she looked at Tara as if realizing that she hadn't

been paying much attention to her. "That's a nice idea, dear. Yes, go get them and we'll see how well you do."

"Aww…look at me and Peggy Dunphy," Gramma said as she turned to the first page. "She was my best friend, you know. We left Cape Breton and went to Brantford together during the war. We had so much fun together, her and I. We worked at the factory and lived at the Women's Residence, and every night we'd go out dancing and we'd meet all kinds of soldiers who were in training. Those were the days…I was so excited about my life at the time, and dreamed of meeting a nice man and getting married and having a family.

"And there's me and Katie. At the time, I was dating Frank Larion. Did you know I dated Frank before Katie married him? We loved each other, but I couldn't marry him because I was a Catholic and he was a Protestant. Daddy would have had my hide if I had married him. Katie didn't care, though, she thought he was handsome, so she married him instead.

"Oh, and there's me and Reg. I think Frank and Katie felt bad that I was single, so they set me up with Reg. We had a lot of fun together, he and I. See. Here's a picture of all of us in Turkey Point on a boat ride. I'll never forget that day." She lingered on that picture for a while.

Tara was confused. "Gramma, I don't get it. Do you like Reg or are you mad at Reg?" Tara had heard all of these stories before, many times, but she still couldn't get over the fact that Reg hadn't wanted to be her mom's father. Tara thought the family didn't like him, so she couldn't understand why Gramma still had fond memories of him.

"Well, dear, as you know, only married people should have babies, and I wanted to marry Reg but he didn't want to marry me. I was so heartbroken when I found out I was pregnant and he wanted nothing to do with me or my baby—I didn't even put his name on Cathy's birth certificate. I was upset for a long time, but eventually I just tried to get over it. So I guess I will always be angry with him about that, but I just can't forget the good times we had before I got pregnant."

It seemed to Tara that after talking to both her mom and Gramma that there was really nothing else to say about Reg Larion. He wasn't going to be playing a role in their lives, he wasn't going to try to have a relationship with her mom, and they wouldn't be heading off to Brantford anytime soon to meet him. So Tara decided that she would stop asking about him and not be curious about him anymore. She felt now that she was more interested in what it was like for Gramma when she had to take care of her baby all alone.

"Was it hard to have a baby all by yourself, Gramma?"

"I tried my best to raise Cathy on my own, you know, but it was next to impossible to find care for her while I worked. Believe it or not, it was difficult to even find a place to live. Most places wouldn't accept a single woman with a baby. I was lucky enough to live with a nice lady named Mrs. Edwards, but in the end I had to ask Mama to take care of my Cathy-O so that I could find a better job and a bigger place to live. I wanted to do the right thing for my daughter."

"Did you miss her when she lived with Nana?" Tara asked. Tara knew how much her mom missed her when she went to summer camp, even if it was just for two weeks, so she couldn't imagine any mother not seeing their child for such a long time.

"Oh, I missed Cathy the whole time. I missed her terribly. It took me three years to move to Stratford, find a job, and to find a place to live. It went by like a flash, but I knew Cathy was happy with Mama and Daddy. I thought that Cathy was so young that she wouldn't even notice three years passing, but maybe it was too long. Maybe she got too used to Mama and so she thought I was a stranger. I thought Cathy would be happy to live with me again. I wanted to give her a better life in Ontario, and I was her mother so I thought it was best that she came with me."

She closed the photo album and reached for her pack of cigarettes. She lit one and exhaled, smoke wafting up to the ceiling.

"I know your mom goes on about Mrs. Wrenn, and her house wasn't the perfect place to live, but it was all I could afford at the time." Gramma was fidgeting with her cigarette pack.

"Gramma, you know how upset Mom gets every time she talks about Mrs. Wrenn, right? I mean, it must have been really bad for her living there. I've always wondered, if it was so bad for her, why didn't you move out?"

"Well, like I said before, I was working hard and trying to find a nice man to take care of us. I felt like I was doing my best, and I just couldn't deal with your mom's complaints about Mrs. Wrenn. I mean, I didn't know what to do, so I just did nothing, I guess."

Tara felt nervous asking so many questions about Mrs. Wrenn because often Gramma would change the subject or go on about something else. But Tara wanted to keep this conversation going to try to find out more about the situation at Mrs. Wrenn's. "But, don't you think it's weird that Mom's still mad at Mrs. Wrenn?"

"Well, yes, I do. It was so many years ago, Tara. Why does she want to go on so much about the past?" Gramma asked. "It feels like she just *wants* to be mad at Mrs. Wrenn."

Tara wanted to ask her next question, but was worried that she'd hurt Gramma's feelings. She took a deep breath—it was now or never. "Gramma, do you think maybe she's mad at you?"

"Why would she be mad at me? She knows that I did everything I could to take care of her."

"But did you listen to her? Did you spend time with her? I just keep thinking about how much I love being with you, and I wonder if Mom felt the same way. And I see you with all the kids you babysit, and I see how much you love them and take care of them, and I wonder if you were like that with Mom when she was little."

Gramma looked out the window, and after a few long moments, she sighed. "I think...I think that I was very sad during those years, Tara. I think I felt like I had let my parents down. And to be honest, I think I let myself down. I made some decisions that I wasn't proud of, and those decisions held me back from living the kind of life that I wanted. When I got Cathy back again, I just wanted to be a good mother to her. I wanted her to love me, but I think I was struggling with the guilty feelings I had about giving her up in the first place."

She pulled a few tissues out of the box and wiped her eyes before tucking them up under her sweater sleeve. Taking a deep breath, she said, "I thought that if I could just get married and give her a father, and a nice house to live in, that maybe she would love me as much as she loved Mama. But I could always tell when I looked into her eyes that she didn't love me like that. She looked at me like she was disappointed in me, and it broke my heart to see that in her eyes. So, maybe I avoided looking at her. Maybe I avoided listening to her because I didn't want to hear that I was a failure. After a while, I started feeling real bad about myself because I couldn't even find a man who wanted to marry me. I think I was desperate and scared and I couldn't handle Cathy seeing that in me."

She paused for a moment. "But, you know, none of that was Cathy's fault, and I wonder now that if I wasn't so preoccupied with finding a husband, I would have given Cathy more attention and listened to her when she was upset about Mrs. Wrenn. Whether Mrs. Wrenn was actually horrible or not doesn't really matter, does it? It was that Cathy *felt* that she was. But I guess what was worse was that she felt like I didn't care."

Gramma buried her face in her hands. "My God, do you think that's why Cathy is always so uncomfortable around me? Why she always seems mad at me? I thought she was just mad at Mrs. Wrenn this whole time, but now I realize that maybe it's actually me she's mad at."

Tara wished that her mom was here to hear all of this. It all made so much sense, and Tara could see that both Gramma and her mom were broken-hearted for their own reasons. But they never talked about it, so neither of them knew how the other felt.

"I don't know if she's mad, Gramma…but I think she's really sad. Do you think you could talk to Mom and let her know how you feel? Maybe tell her that you wish you could fix it?"

"Well, I can't go back in time and fix the past, dear. I think we just have to forget the past and get on with life. There's no use in talking about things that are depressing."

"But, Gramma, you don't have to go back to the past, you could just tell her you're sorry and that you wish things had been different."

"I don't know, Tara, your mom gets pretty angry when I talk about anything like that. I think it might be better to just be nice and talk about things that aren't sad, and then we don't have to be upset."

Tara felt frustrated. It would be so simple to just have a conversation. *Doesn't everyone always feel better when they say they're sorry?* It seemed easy to Tara, so she couldn't understand why Gramma thought it would be better to ignore it.

A week later, both Tara and her mother were back at home. They were sitting at the kitchen table discussing how their week apart had been.

"How was the trip, Mom?" Tara asked. "Was Nana OK on the plane?"

"Oh, my dear God in Heaven, it was not an easy flight, but I was so relieved when me and Marlene finally got her settled into Big Molly's house. All the stress of being at Avon Crest and taking that plane all the way to Cape Breton drained right out of Nana the moment she got to Big Molly's. We got her all set up with a doctor, arranged for nurses to come in once a day, got the paperwork she needed done, and then we headed home. I have to say, I feel exhausted now and like I can't think anymore. I just want to get back to normal. How did it go at Gramma's?"

Tara did notice that her mom looked a little pale, which is what happened to her when she was worried and missing sleep. She didn't know if now was a good time to bring up the conversation she'd had with Gramma, but Tara wanted so badly for them to have a better relationship, she couldn't wait.

"Mom, I talked to Gramma about Mrs. Wrenn and how miserable you felt when you lived there."

Her mom pressed her lips together and went to the kitchen counter to plug the kettle in.

"I think Gramma feels bad, Mom. She feels bad that you weren't happy there."

"She feels bad, does she? What does she feel bad about? Leaving me there with that horrible woman all day long? Not coming home until late at night so that if I wasn't cleaning Mrs. Wrenn's kitchen or oiling her baseboards, I was alone most of the time? Does she feel bad about kissing her stupid boyfriend right on the same bed that I was sleeping in?"

"I think she's sorry that she made some bad decisions, and that—"

"Bad decisions? I'd say she made some bad decisions. The worst ones were keeping me in the first place, and then taking me away from Nana. How could she take me away from her?

She's the only person I ever loved, and she took me away and gave me to Mrs. Wrenn instead!"

"But Mom, I—"

"I can't talk about this anymore, Tara. All I can think about is poor Nana on her goddamned death bed, and there's Mom feeling sorry for herself and defending all the things she did and didn't do. I have no patience for her right now, and I don't want to hear anything more about it."

Later that night, while Tara was lying in bed, she realized that there was nothing else she could do. She'd thought if she could talk to Gramma, and then talk to Mom, she could somehow fix their relationship. But with Gramma being depressed and taking so many pills, and her mom going out of her mind with worry about Nana, Tara felt helpless. Maybe she needed to understand that some relationships couldn't be fixed. That people are damaged and hurt and can't see how to get out of it. Maybe Tara had to realize that, just because she loved her mom and grandmother more than anything, it may never be possible for them to love each other the same way.

Suddenly, she felt tired and just wanted to close her eyes. Maybe this problem was too grown up for her to understand.

CHAPTER SIXTEEN

April 1984—Easter: The Big Fight

Nana was gone.

Tara couldn't believe it. She'd died on the fifteenth of March and had been buried on St. Patrick's Day, of all days. It was either really good luck or really bad luck that she'd been buried on the Barron family's most revered day of the year.

Nana had only been given three months to live when she left Stratford in September, and she'd fought hard and made it until after Christmas. But, in late February, she'd taken a turn for the worse. When they'd known the end was near, Gramma and two of her brothers, Doug and Mickey, had gone to Cape Breton to see their mother for the last time. They spent two weeks visiting her in the hospital, sitting by her bed, and holding her hand. She was still holding on, but she wasn't getting better and they all knew she was near the end. Eventually, they had decided to return home and Tara knew it must have been gut-wrenching for Gramma to leave Nana's side. There were times when Nana had been disappointed with Gramma, and times when Gramma had been frustrated with Nana, but they'd had a special bond—Gramma had been her first-born, after all.

In early March, Tara's mom and Aunt Marlene had gone to Cape Breton again to join Janey and the rest of the family at Nana's side. Nana talked non-stop. She talked about the doctors and the pain she was in, she talked about her children and her grandchildren and her great-grandchildren, and she talked about her brothers and sisters and her parents and her life as a little girl.

She was the last of her siblings to go, and she'd said she was looking forward to seeing them all in Heaven. She'd held her rosary and she prayed and she asked for the priest almost every day until finally she said she was ready, she'd had enough, and she passed away peacefully with her family by her side.

Now, it was Sunday, April 22, 1984, and the family was trying to celebrate Easter at Gramma's. Only a few had come for dinner: Tara and her mom, Joanie and Stan, Marlene and Shawn, and of course Big Joe and Joey. But it was a quick meal and everyone left early—Joey went out with his friends, and Big Joe went to the Legion—so it was just Tara and her mom left to help Gramma with the dishes.

Tara didn't especially like being alone with just Gramma and Mom. She always felt she had to start a conversation, and bring up something they could all talk about that wouldn't cause tension. But today that was next to impossible.

Gramma had gone to the cupboard several times to get something out of a pill bottle, and her mom was on her second glass of white wine. Tara thought that maybe they should just head home, but her mother kept going around and around, cleaning and tidying the kitchen and the living room, until she finally made her way over to Nana's rocking chair.

She stopped and stared at Nana's empty seat. Her heating pad was still hung over the back of the chair and her prayer books were still sitting on the little table.

Her mom had started gathering up the prayer books when Gramma came into the living room and said, "No, please don't, Cathy. I want to leave them there. It makes me feel like maybe Mama isn't really gone…that she'll be back soon to read her books and say her prayers."

"Well, Mom, I was there when she died so I can tell you that she's definitely not coming back here."

"I may have already left Cape Breton when she died, Cathy, and maybe you don't remember that I was there for two weeks, sitting by her side, but I *was* there." Gramma sat down in her chair while she watched her daughter sink into Nana's rocking chair.

Nana had an old white shawl that she kept draped over the rocking chair to keep her back warm, and Tara's mom took it and held it against her chest. No one said anything for a few minutes.

"How I wish I could still talk to her," Gramma said. "There were so many things I wanted to say."

Tara's mother looked up, for once interested in something Gramma had so say.

"But she's gone now, so I guess I may as well accept the fact. Maybe I'll just think she's at Big Molly's, and as long as I believe that, I'll be OK," Gramma said.

"But she's not at Big Molly's, Mom, she's gone. Why do you always do that?"

Gramma started fidgeting. "Do what?"

"Do that thing where you just ignore the issue, pretend it doesn't exist, just decide that you don't want to acknowledge it, and then go on your merry way."

"I just don't see what use there is in thinking about the past and feeling depressed about it. You can't change the past, you know, so why go on about it?"

"Because, Mom, sometimes the past and the hurt it causes needs to be dealt with," she said. "Oh, forget about it, you just don't understand."

Tara's mom looked over at the coffee table at Nana's hand mirror. She went over and picked it up and looked at the glass, as if hoping somehow Nana would be in there.

"Well, if you're talking about that Mrs. Wrenn business again, Cathy, I really wish you'd just forget it," Gramma said as she lit a cigarette.

This wasn't going how Tara had hoped it might. Tara thought that maybe Gramma would say she was sorry about her daughter's childhood, and that if she could do it all over again and make it better she would.

"Forget it? Forget it? How could I forget how that woman ruined my childhood."

Oh no, Tara thought. *This is going to be bad.*

"How could I forget that you took me from Nana, the only person I ever truly loved and made me live with that bitch?"

Gramma's eyes grew wide. "Cathy, I know you loved Mama, but I am your mother and it breaks my heart to hear you say you only truly loved one person!"

"Well, you don't have to worry about it because Nana didn't love me back. Not as much as she seemed to love everyone else." She dropped the mirror on the coffee table. "Why is it so damned hard to get anyone to love me?"

"*I* love you, Cathy!" Gramma cried.

"How could you love me when you let Mrs. Wrenn be so mean to me? I told you over and over all the wretched things she did to me. How miserable she made me. Don't you remember how she made me eat black pepper? Don't you remember that she ruined Santa Claus for me? Don't you remember that she locked me outside? Don't you remember that she would creep up the stairs every morning to check to see if I was wearing my fucking underpants?"

Gramma was shaking in her chair and her face was pale. "No, Cathy, I don't remember!"

"Why don't you remember? Why didn't you believe me?"

"I was working hard and I was trying to find a husband and I was doing my best!"

Tara knew that wasn't what her mom needed to hear. Her mom always said that Gramma had excuses for everything, that she lived in a fantasy world where everything was fine. She hoped Gramma would take this opportunity to say the magic words, but instead Gramma panicked.

"I thought Mrs. Wrenn was a nice lady, Cathy. She gave you that card when Ronnie was born. I don't know what to say to make you feel better, but I really don't think I did anything wrong!"

Cathy flew across the room and stood over her mother. "Of course you didn't do anything wrong, Mom," she hissed. "I guess I was the crazy one. I exaggerated and made up lies, didn't I? That's the kind of little girl I was, right? Well, if that's the kind of girl I was, why didn't you just leave me at Nana's where I belonged?"

Tara's heart was racing seeing her mom's body shaking and tears streaming down her cheeks. But Tara knew they weren't tears of sadness, they were tears of fury.

Gramma shrank back in her chair, seemingly terrified of what her daughter would do.

Seeing her mother's fear, Cathy stood up and backed away. "Oh, for God's sake, Mom, I'm not going to hurt you." She looked around for her purse. "You're such a friggin' actress! Tara, get your shoes on right this instant!"

Gramma got out of her chair and quickly followed them to the front hall. "Cathy, don't go, don't leave like this. Mrs. Wrenn wasn't that bad, not so bad that you have to act crazy like this!"

If her mother's fury had subsided for a moment, it was back in full force now. Her eyes went black and her lips went white.

"I am not the crazy one," she screamed. She grabbed her purse and flung it toward her mother. "I am leaving this house and I will never darken your fucking door again!"

———— ✦◦✦ ————

In the back seat of the speeding car, and well away from her seething mother, Tara fought back tears. It took a while for her racing heart to finally slow down, and halfway home she felt calm enough to try to process what just happened. Tara thought back to everything she had learned about her mom's childhood, and how she'd been so affected by Mrs. Wrenn. Tara also thought a lot about Gramma, and even through Tara knew Gramma loved her daughter she also knew that Gramma wouldn't—or couldn't—take responsibility for her role in the misery at Mrs. Wrenn's house.

After all these years of spending time at Gramma's, Tara had just wanted to find out two things: why was her mom still so mad at Mrs. Wrenn, and why was her mom so tense around Gramma?

Tara now understood that her mom resented Gramma for taking her away from Nana, and for *not* taking her away from Mrs. Wrenn. Tara also understood that her mom felt like Gramma didn't stick up for her, and that Gramma didn't listen to her. But now Tara wondered if maybe there was more going on in her mom's heart than just hate for Mrs. Wrenn and anger at Gramma.

By the time they'd got back home to Kitchener, and Tara had gone to her room, she felt exhausted. She'd hoped that somehow her mom and Gramma would finally have a chance to make things better, but the situation was far from better and Tara was frustrated and worried because everything seemed to be so much worse.

Tara had tried talking to her mom about all of this before, and she'd thought maybe she could be the one to help them. But as she got ready for bed, she decided again that she had to give up.

Maybe it would be easier to not think about it anymore. Gramma and Mom didn't get along, and that's just the way it was.

Maybe Gramma was right. The past is the past, and there's no use in going on about it.

CHAPTER SEVENTEEN

Summer 1984—The Accident

The day had finally arrived. It was the day of her First Holy Communion, but Tara wasn't excited about it at all.

Most kids got their First Communion in grade two, but because Tara went to a Public school instead of a Catholic school, she hadn't been able to receive it at the appropriate age. Her mom had said that she always felt so disappointed about it because she herself had many fond memories of her own First Communion in Cape Breton with Nana.

By the time Tara was in grade five, her mom had been going back to church more often and had decided that, come hell or high water, Tara would get her First Communion after all. So her mom had registered Tara for correspondence courses run by the nuns at the local diocese, and then went and bought her a dress and some new shoes to go with it. Tara had liked the new outfit, but did not appreciate all the extra reading and homework she'd had to do. When she complained to her mom, her mother had insisted that she just focus and work through it. Her mom said that everyone else in their family was Catholic, so even though Tara didn't go to a Catholic school she'd do what she had to do to make sure her daughter was a good Catholic.

Tara loved going to church with Gramma at St. Joseph's, and wanted to be a Catholic like her and Nana, but the thing she had worried about the most was taking her First Communion with a bunch of seven-year-olds. She was tall and skinny, and even though her dress was pretty Tara knew she'd stick out like a sore thumb when she stood up in front of the priest with the younger kids. But she really did want to get her First Communion, so she put on a smile and made the best of it and before she knew it, she was back at the house celebrating with her family.

Now that the ceremony was over, Tara could relax as her family gathered in their backyard, where her mom had set up chairs on the deck and in the garden. She had laid a beautifully embroidered cloth over the table, where she'd placed vases of fresh flowers, linen napkins, and delicate antique dishes filled with all sorts of homemade appetizers. Her mom was excited to make this day as special as the one she remembered from when she was a little girl, and Tara was excited because Gramma was coming.

Tara hadn't seen Gramma at all since her mom had completely freaked out and screamed at her on that unforgettable Easter Sunday. You would think that, after an episode like that, her mom would stick to her guns and never see Gramma again, but just a few weeks ago Joey had graduated from high school and Mom said she wouldn't miss it for the world—even if Gramma would be there.

Apparently the whole day had been awkward and uncomfortable, and her mom said that Gramma had acted like nothing was wrong—as if her daughter had never screamed at her and threatened to "never darken her door again." She said she'd tried to avoid talking to Gramma, but when she finally had to she kept the conversation to a minimum. Her mom also said she didn't have the energy to keep being angry at Gramma, and it was easier to just be civil and get it over with.

Tara wondered if maybe that was for the best. If her mom had something else bottled up inside her, something she wasn't willing to let out, maybe the best thing for them both was to just be polite at family get-togethers and move on. Tara was looking forward to seeing Gramma, but she worried that Gramma would feel uncomfortable being here in Kitchener with Mom and the rest of the family.

Tara looked up just as Gramma and Joey made their way down the stairs from the driveway and into the yard. Gramma waved at Tara, while Joey made a beeline for the appetizers.

"Hi, Tara. You look pretty as a picture," Gramma said as she walked carefully across the grass toward where Tara was sitting. "I'm so proud of you, dear, for getting your First Holy Communion."

"Thanks, Gramma. I'm happy you're here." Tara stood up and gave Gramma a gentle hug. "I've been missing you."

"I've been missing you too, dear. I must say I'm always a little happier when I'm around you," Gramma said, her voice wavering. "Let's sit down so I can put my feet up. I still have this darned blood clot in my ankle and I'm feeling a little shaky."

"Do you want me to get you a drink first?" Tara asked. "Or something to eat?"

"Just one of those cold beers your mom has in the cooler over there will do it, dear," Gramma said as she eased her way into a chair. "Are you going to get yourself a pop or something?"

Tara and Gramma settled down with their drinks and Tara listened as Gramma talked.

"Did you know that my Joey graduated a few weeks ago? The ceremony took place at the Festival Theatre. Imagine! He's going to grade thirteen, and then off to university. It seems like yesterday that I was rocking him to sleep. The time sure flies, doesn't it? Anyway, the whole thing was marvelous to see. The school band played, and all the boys were dressed in nice suits, and the girls looked lovely too. I was so proud of him."

Tara thought Gramma had seemed a bit nervous when she'd first arrived, but talking seemed to have calmed her down so Tara patiently listened while Gramma continued.

"Of course, I'm missing Mama every day. And it's real sad on Saturdays, when I remember how I used to put the record player on. She liked to listen to Bing Crosby and Harry Hibbs—but she's gone now," she said, wiping her eyes with a tissue. "I do wish Mama was still here."

"I know, Gramma, so do I," Tara said. "I loved when the three of us listened to records and you would sing along. You knew all the words to all the songs."

Gramma nodded, took a sip of beer, and continued. "So, instead of playing records, I just do my work, read a little, and go for a short walk. Because it's not healthy thinking of the past, you know, Tara. Whenever I feel myself getting depressed about the past I just go upstairs, have a shower and wash my hair, and then go uptown to the library or somewhere."

She paused for a minute to fish a cigarette out of her purse. "Anyway, did you know that I had another birthday on June fourteenth? I sure wished you could have been there, Tara. We had such a nice time. Joanie and Stan came over with Doug and Elsie, and they brought me a cake and a lovely card. I can't believe I'm sixty years old now."

She exhaled smoke into the light breeze "But I guess you're only as old as you feel, and I don't feel old. So, as long as I keep thinking that way I'll be OK."

Tara told Gramma all about her year in grade five, and about her friends and her dance class and how her mom had signed her up to go to summer camp again this year. "My friend Jenny is sad that I'm going away, but I told her that it's just for the last two weeks of July and that I'd be back in two shakes of a lamb's tail."

"Ha! That's what I always say, Tara." Gramma patted Tara's knee. "Now you say it—that's so cute!"

"Supper's ready." Tara's mom was calling from the kitchen window. "Everyone come in and eat while it's still hot!"

"Cathy! This supper was just perfect," Gramma said as they all finished their meal. "Everything was so delicious."

"Umm…thanks," her mom mumbled as she started clearing plates. "OK, everyone, let's go outside and get some pictures of Tara before the sun sets."

Tara had no hope that her mom and grandmother would have any meaningful conversation, but at least there wasn't any yelling or taking off in the car. And maybe, like Tara, her mom and Gramma realized it was best to leave it alone and just get along for the sake of the family.

⁂

Now that her First Communion was over, Tara could concentrate on the last two weeks of school before summer vacation began.

Tara and her friend Jenny had lots of plans for the next two weeks, and were going to hang out every day after school in Tara's backyard. Their goal was to get as tanned as possible so that when they went to the pool with their friends they would win the tanning competition that only the two of them knew about. And they also wanted to work on the air-band song they were planning on performing on the last day of school.

Normally, Tara had to go to Becky's house next door until her mom got home from work, but Becky would often let her hang out with Jenny in Tara's backyard. A few weeks earlier, Ronnie had told Tara about a place in the forest behind their house where some older kids had built a tree house. Tara loved climbing, and loved the forest, so one day after school, instead of their planned tanning session she asked Jenny to go with her to find the tree house.

It only crossed her mind for a minute that she should maybe ask Becky if she was allowed to play in the forest, but excitement got the best of her and she conveniently forgot about needing permission.

"C'mon, Jenny, I have something really cool to show you and I think I know exactly where it is. Follow me!"

The girls ran down the back steps and through the garden, jumped over the narrow creek that ran across the backyard, stepped over the fallen trees and branches and crooked limbs, then walked for about ten minutes until they came upon the tree house.

All up the trunk, someone had nailed small pieces of wood that acted as rungs. They were nailed in the middle, and Tara knew that meant that they would wobble from side to side when she stepped on them. This was the sort of thing she'd learned while climbing around at her dad's barn.

"Let's try it," she said to Jenny. "Give me a boost."

"It seems too high, Tara. I don't think we should go all the way to the top."

Tara looked up. As far as she could see, the rickety wooden rungs went up the trunk and disappeared into the leaves. She could just barely make out the floor of the tree house, and she could tell that someone had built walls and a bit of a roof.

"Boost me up, Jenny, so I can check it out."

Up she went, one rung at a time, taking care not to put too much weight on one side or the other, until finally she made it to the base of the tree house. There was a square hole cut into the floorboards so she could hoist herself inside. She was safely sitting on the wooden floor, although it was more like a platform because there were actually only two walls and the rest was open.

She looked down through the hole and could barely see Jenny standing at the foot of the tree, looking up at her. *Wow,*

I'm really high up, she thought. *This might even be higher than the top of the barn.*

She called down to Jenny. "Come up! There's room for both of us."

When Jenny, breathless, reached the top, Tara took her hand and helped her get situated on the floor. "Tara, oh my Gawd, this is way too high. We shouldn't be up here. My parents would kill me if they knew I was up this high."

"Yeah, but this is so neat! We're right in the trees, and there are probably squirrels and birds and maybe raccoons and things up here. Maybe if we sing, they'll come in and play with us."

"Are you crazy, Tara? The last thing I want is for a stinkin' raccoon to come and 'play' with us way up here!"

Tara slowly stood up and carefully walked over to the edge of the platform. She wanted to see how cool things looked from up here. But all she could see were green leaves and brown branches; she couldn't even see the ground. She saw a large limb growing out from the trunk, out over the platform and above their heads. If she could just climb onto the limb, she could shimmy her way out past the branches to see if it gave a better view.

"What are you doing?" Jenny sounded alarmed seeing what Tara was up to.

"I'm just going to crawl out a bit to see what I can see," Tara said, already in the midst of hoisting herself up and over the limb.

"Oh my Gawd, Tara! Come back down. You're going to fall!"

Ignoring Jenny, Tara inched her way along the limb. There were just a few more inches to go until she got to the spot that she thought would be far enough. She was just about to turn back and smile triumphantly at Jenny when she heard the ear-splitting crack of the limb breaking behind her.

All Tara was aware of after hearing the crack, was the quiet and the dark. A few minutes later she could hear something in the distance, a high-pitched sound from far away. When she focused on where she was, and what she was doing, Tara could tell she was lying on the forest floor. She could feel soft moss at her sides. Her eyes were closed, but flashing through her mind over and over again was the image of green leaves speeding past her face and the sound of branches snapping as she'd broken through them. She tried opening her eyes to erase the image, but they were too heavy. She decided instead to focus on the sound that was growing louder. It had been far away, but it was coming closer now. She listened. Then she realized that it was Jenny, screaming.

"Oh my Gawd, Oh my Gawd, Oh my Gawd!"

She tried to focus on Jenny's voice to take away the sound of breaking branches. Her head cleared a bit more and she tried to sit up. But as soon as she did, she felt dizzy and thought maybe she'd be sick.

Jenny cried out, kneeling beside her. "Oh my Gawd, lay down. Lay down!"

Tara lied back down and tried to speak. "Get Becky," she said in a whisper.

"What? What, Tara? Oh my Gawd, there's so much blood. What should I do?"

"Go get Becky. My neighbour," Tara said again.

The next thing she knew, she was on a stretcher in her driveway. When she finally opened her eyes all she could see were red and blue lights swirling around her head.

"Careful, now, she might have broken her neck. Get the brace."

"Try to stop the bleeding on her face. Looks like her teeth got smashed out, and there is a laceration running from the side of her mouth to her chin. Probably two or three inches. She'll need plastic surgery for that."

"OK, her arm is definitely broken in a few places so let's get that secure. Oh wait, shit. I think we have a puncture here. Yep, her left lung. Gotta get in a tube in there right away."

Who are they talking about, Tara wondered. She felt dizzy, but she wasn't in any pain. She was certain that whoever they were talking about must be hurt pretty bad.

Suddenly, she heard her mother's voice. "What's happening?" Her voice grew shrill. "What's HAPPENING?"

"Someone grab the mother…she's going to faint. Is this your mother, son? Can you find a place for her to sit?"

"Is that my sister? Holy shit, is that my little sister?"

Tara heard Ronnie's voice coming closer.

"Step away, son, while we get her loaded. Tell your mom to get someone to follow us to Emergency at St Mary's Hospital. This little girl needs attention right away."

Tara could sense the darkness closing in on her again, and she realized she could no longer feel anything. She couldn't hear her mom or brother's voices anymore, so she let herself sink into the quiet and the dark.

CHAPTER EIGHTEEN

Summer 1984—The Hospital

When Tara became aware again, she knew that she was cold and she was wet.

She was also aware that she was in a hospital and that she was lying in a bed. Someone had washed her but had forgotten to dry her. She fell back out of consciousness. She woke up again. She was cold. She was wet. *Could someone dry me please? And cover me with a blanket?*

"Nurse." Tara's voice was a whisper. Her lips could hardly move. "Nurse?" No one was coming and she was so cold. She tried again. "Nurse!"

Suddenly, she couldn't breathe.

"Now, now, I'm here. Just relax and only take very shallow breaths," said the nurse who had rushed to her side, soothing her.

Tara could hear her tsk when the nurse saw that Tara had been washed but not dried off, and left without any blankets. "She must have gone on break," the nurse said, muttering to herself.

Tara then felt the nurse cover her with a warm, heavy blanket. She tucked it in around the sides and plumped up her pillow. "You've had quite an accident, Tara. The paramedics said you fell forty feet out of a tree house. Your neighbour called nine-one-one and the fire department had to get you out of the forest and onto your driveway so the paramedics could treat you. You're very lucky to be alive."

"What is wrong with me? I can't talk right, and I can't breathe right."

"I'll let your mom explain all of that to you. She's just down the hall in the waiting room," the nurse said as she checked the chart on the clipboard and the level of the fluid in the IV bag. "I'll go and get her now. You just relax and try not to breathe too deeply."

Tara's mom rushed into the room and over to Tara's side. Tara had never seen her mom look like this before. Her face was a mixture of horror, dread, shock, anxiety, love, and heartbreak. Tara watched as her mom tried to comfort her. She could tell that her mom wanted to hold her hands, but one had a cast on it and the other was full of tubes and tape. Her mom clearly wanted to kiss her cheek, but she must have worried that she'd brush the quick and messy stitches that kept her daughter's face together. Her mom also wouldn't want to kiss and hurt her mouth, where the nurse had said five of her teeth were broken off at the gum line. Her mom wouldn't want to hug her because she wouldn't want to disturb the one-inch tube that was slowly inflating Tara's lung, and she might have worried about holding Tara's head in her arms because of her fractured jaw and skull.

So her mom just stood there, her eyes welling up. She held on to Tara's foot and squeezed hard, tears running down her cheeks. "God almighty, little girl. What the heck were you doing so high up in a tree! When we came home and we saw those ambulance lights in our driveway, we were scared to death!"

"Am I in trouble, Mom?" Tara worried that her mom was mad that she'd gone into the forest without permission.

"My goodness, Tara, you are not in trouble. But you could have died, for God's sake!"

"Why can't I breathe right?"

"It's called a punctured lung, which means that you have a hole in your lung—or some sort of trauma from the impact of the fall—and now they have to blow it back up again and the hole has to heal. You'll be alright, but you can't breathe deeply for now so try not to talk too much."

"I can't talk right either."

"Well, little girl, you have a big cut on your face and you lost some teeth, but you're OK. We'll make sure you get surgery and everything else you'll need for your teeth, but for now just relax and get some rest. When you wake up I'll be sitting right here beside you, and I'm going to stay all night to make sure you're comfortable."

"My arm hurts and my face hurts and my head hurts and there's a bad taste in my mouth."

"I'll call the nurse to get you more pain medication, and your mouth is yucky because you still have a lot of blood in there. They want to wait until you're stable enough to take a look at your mouth, your tongue, and your teeth. But here, I'll get a warm cloth and wipe some of that dried blood off your lips."

Tara felt sleepy and sore and, without waiting for the nurse to come back, she fell asleep, comforted knowing that her mom would be there when she woke up.

Tara was in the intensive care unit for seven days. Her mom was there all day, every day, but after the first night she had to go home after visiting hours. Some days Ronnie or Tara's stepdad came to see her, and some days it was Aunt Marlene. But mostly it was just her mom there, giving her water, bathing her with a soft cloth, calling the nurse when she was needed, and making sure Tara was warm and comfortable.

After a week, and on the first day that her mother had to go back to work, the doctors said Tara could be transferred to the ward upstairs. When the nurse came in, he explained to Tara that he had to pick her up and carry her from one bed to the other.

"Oh, you don't have to do that. I can stand up," Tara said, perplexed that he thought she couldn't get up by herself.

"Well, you've been in that bed for a week and you'd be surprised how weak your muscles have gotten."

What he didn't know was that Tara was a competitive dancer, and there was no way her muscles were so weak that she couldn't stand.

"Can I *try* to stand on my own?" she asked.

He smiled. "You can try if you want to, but I'll be right here in case you need me."

Tara swung her legs over the side of the bed and placed her bare feet on the floor. The nurse held her hands, and as soon as she put weight on her legs she collapsed. She would have fallen onto the floor if he hadn't caught her.

"See? Hard to believe, isn't it?" He picked her up and gently placed her in the new bed, then wheeled her down the hall, into the elevator, and up to her new room on the third floor.

"There you go, young lady," he said once he got her settled. "Your mom is waiting down the hall, so I'll go tell her that you're ready for visitors."

When her mom came in she made sure that Tara had everything she needed, that she had an extra blanket, that her pillow was in the right position, and that she wasn't in any pain.

"I feel pretty good, Mom. Where did all these flowers come from?" Tara thought maybe the patient who'd been in here before had left their flowers behind.

"They're all for you, little girl." Her mom started repositioning vases and greeting cards and wrapped gifts. "For the past week all the people who love you have been sending these gifts, hoping they would make you feel better. When the nurses found out what room you'd be in they put all these things out for you. Isn't that sweet?"

Tara couldn't get over it. There must have been ten vases of flowers, all kinds of stuffed toys, and piles of cards.

"Can I read them, Mom?" Tara asked, sitting up in her bed.

"Of course! Open them all up." Her mom handed her a stack of cards.

She'd got cards from all her friends at school, and even one from her teacher. Actually, there were cards from several of her past teachers. There were also some from the neighbours on their street, and Aunt Marlene and Janey and Gramma, and even one from a stranger who'd seen an article about her accident in the newspaper.

Tara was surprised to find out that a reporter had written about her accident. "Was I really in the newspaper, Mom?"

"Oh, yes. It's turned into a big deal. The fire department had to go into the forest with chainsaws and cut the tree down. They said that it was a hazard, and they didn't want anyone else to hurt themselves trying to climb it. The firemen said that they'd never seen a tree house built so high. No can believe that you're still alive…you really are a lucky girl."

Later that day her stepdad came in with a big carton of ice cream, and Ronnie and his friend came to visit too. Before her mom left for the evening, she let Tara know that Gramma and Big Joe were coming the next day.

"Oh, that's good! Was Gramma upset when you told her I fell out of the tree?"

"Was she upset? My God, she was beside herself! When I told her what happened to you, she dropped the phone. I could hear her gasping—it sounded like she was in pain, and I was worried she was having a heart attack or something. It was a full minute 'til she came back on the phone, but she was crying so hard she couldn't hold it! Usually she gets teary when she's upset, but I've never seen or heard her cry like that before. Anyway, after I told her about all your injuries, she said that she would ask all the priests, the monsignor, the deacon, the sisters, and even the housekeepers at both St. Joseph's and Immaculate Conception to say a prayer for you. She thinks it's a miracle that you're alive."

The next day, when Gramma and Big Joe walked into her room, Tara's throat tightened and she felt like she wanted to cry. All of a sudden, she felt like a very little girl.

"Oh, my dear God in Heaven, Tara, you scared the living daylights out of us," Gramma said as she came over to the bed and carefully tried to hug Tara.

The doctors had removed the tube from Tara's lung, so she could breathe more easily now. The IV had also been removed because she could eat on her own, but she still had the cast and it was heavy and made it hard to hug people.

"Tara. What you do? Why you go up that tree?" Big Joe asked from where he was standing. "You think you are monkey?

"Now, Joe, she's not a monkey, she's just a very curious young lady who likes to climb things. But, Tara, please promise me that you'll never do something like that again." Before Tara could answer, Gramma continued. "I was sitting in my chair and I kept thinking to myself that something was wrong, that something was just not right, and then your mom called to tell me you fell out of a tree. It's just like that, isn't it? One minute it seems like you're happy, and then something turns up that makes you sad, right? When my Cathy phoned to tell me the news, I said to myself, 'Can you imagine? The poor little girl, she's such a sweet, lovable thing. I'll have to get everyone I know to pray that she gets better.' And I knew that, with time and prayer, you'd be OK."

"Rita, you talk too much. She getting tired. Let's get coffee and let her sleep."

"Alright, Joe," Gramma said, flapping her hand at him. "Now, Tara, you have a sleep and we'll be right back. Is your mother down in the cafeteria? She's probably having a hot cup of tea. We'll go and find her." She kissed Tara on the cheek and she and Big Joe made their way out of the room.

Tara was so happy that Gramma and Big Joe had made the trip to Kitchener to come and see her, but Big Joe was right: she was starting to feel tired and she thought she'd close her eyes for a few minutes.

Sometime later, she was just coming out of a deep sleep when she realized that her mom and Gramma had come back into the room and were talking quietly. Big Joe must have decided to stay in the cafeteria.

Tara realized they were talking in a pretty serious tone, so she kept her eyes closed and pretended to still be asleep. She wanted to hear what they were saying to each other.

"When I saw Tara on that stretcher in the driveway, and I saw all the blood and the neck brace and the tubes and everything, I just about died," her mom said. "How could that be my little girl? How could that be Tara? Of course, I blamed myself for not being there, but you know what's crazy? I wasn't there because I had to take Ronnie to this very same hospital to get his cast off from when he broke his wrist at baseball practice." She paused, then continued. "We were driving down the road toward the house when Ronnie said, 'What are all those blinking lights? That's not our house, is it?' Then, when we realized that it was, we were both in shock."

"Oh, my God, hun, I bet you were in shock alright," said Gramma.

"That first night in the ICU, when I stayed with her all night, I just kept thinking over and over again what would happen to me if Tara didn't make it. I kept thinking about how much I love her, and what I could have done differently to protect her."

Tara wondered if her mom was actually speaking to Gramma, or if she was just talking out loud.

"Somehow I knew that Tara was going to be OK. But, ever since then, I've had this nagging feeling that I have to change my life somehow."

Her mom stopped talking and went quiet for a few minutes.

"What, Cathy? What do you have to change?" Gramma asked.

Normally, Gramma didn't ask her mom deep sorts of questions like this, but she must have been feeling comfortable enough. Maybe it was because her mother was actually just sitting there and talking freely, not busying herself with small tasks like she normally would do when she was around Gramma.

"For myself, and for my kids, I have to find a way to have more joy in my life," Cathy said, her soft voice growing stronger. "I have to be happier."

"Now that sounds like a good idea, Cathy."

Tara knew Gramma wouldn't want to say too much so she could be sure she didn't say the wrong thing.

"But you know, I'm not sure if I've ever actually been happy."

"Oh, hun, you've been happy before. I've seen it," said Gramma.

"No...I don't think I've ever been truly happy, Mom. Some good things have happened to me, like having Ronnie and Tara, but something's always held me back from actually feeling the way I should feel. And I think it has to do with Mrs. Wrenn."

Tara could imagine Gramma freezing and holding her breath. She knew that any time talk of Mrs. Wrenn came up, the conversation always ended badly.

"I need to figure out why I keep going back to that time of my life. It was five years that we lived there with her, and that's a long time, but I have to figure out how to let it go."

Gramma was silent. She must have known it would be best to not say anything and just listen.

"When I told you about Tara's accident, Mom, you were so upset. At first I felt a pang of jealousy because I never felt you had that sort of emotion about me, but then I realized how very much you care about her. She's your granddaughter and you really love her a lot, don't you?"

"With all my heart and soul, Cathy." Gramma's voice cracked. "But I love you just the same, you know."

"Do you? I've never felt that there was any sort of bond between us."

"Well, of course I do...and, yes, we have a bond, don't we? Why do you think I don't love you?"

"To be honest, I don't think I've ever trusted you. I feel like you've never defended me."

"But, Cathy, I..."

"No, Mom. Let's stop talking about it for now because we just keep going around and around. But I am going to figure out how to let go of the pain Mrs. Wrenn caused me. It's something I have to do."

Tara secretly smiled to herself. She didn't know exactly what this meant, but to hear her mother talk so calmly to Gramma, and to know that Gramma hadn't said any of those things that drove her mom nuts made her feel like something good might happen. She opened her eyes as her mom and Gramma made their way over to her bedside.

"Hi, Mom. Hi, Gramma."

———————◦⟨∞⟩◦———————

The next several days went by fast. A girl a bit older than her had some sort of surgery and was now her roommate. Her name was Suzy, and she was very nice. Her family got her a TV, so the girls would watch some of their favourite shows. They talked all day about their schools, their friends, and what they liked to do in the summer. Tara was sad to say that she couldn't go to summer camp this year because of the accident.

"I normally go to camp the last two weeks of July, but I won't be better in time so my mom had to cancel my registration. That's the only time I've cried since being here; when I found out that I couldn't go to camp."

The very next day, Tara was in for a big surprise.

She looked up from the colouring she was doing when she realized that three teenagers were standing in the doorway to her room. It was three of her favourite camp counsellors! Tara thought they looked funny being here in a hospital room instead of out at camp.

"Oh my God, what are you guys doing here?" Tara sat up and quickly put her colouring away.

"Hi, Tara!" They spoke in unison as they rushed over to her side of the room and arranged themselves around her bed.

"When we found out what happened to you we all felt just horrible," said the one with the short brown hair. "All the counsellors remember you, and we know how much you love camp. We were so sad when we found out that you couldn't make it this summer, so we wanted to come and visit you."

"We were hoping you could somehow come to camp later this summer," said the taller girl with long blond hair. "But, when we looked at the rest of the schedule, we realized that we're going to be totally full."

"So, we talked to our director and guess what?" asked the third girl, who always gave the best hugs. "He said that he could create a space just for you to come in August! Would you like that?"

Tara couldn't say a word. She swallowed hard and blinked back the tears that were threatening to fall. *Are they really here to visit me and to tell me that they have a spot for me?*

"Are you serious?" she asked, tears escaping and streaming down her face.

"We're serious! You're one of our favourite campers and we just couldn't let the summer go by without having you there!"

The girls hugged Tara before they left and, for hours afterward, Tara's heart felt like it was about to burst. She would never forget them and their visit for as long as she lived.

Another few days had passed and her fractures had healed, the swelling had gone down, and she could breathe normally. Tara was finally allowed to go home!

For the first little while, she had to lie on the rec room couch because she didn't quite have her energy back, but at least she could watch First Choice Superchannel all day. She tended to watch the same two movies over and over: "North Country" and "The Pirate Movie." Her mom had to be at work during the day, so Tara made herself peanut butter and jam sandwiches, played with her cats and dogs, and watched more of her favourite movies. She had lost thirteen pounds while she was in the hospital, so she ate as many sandwiches as she could. And whenever the sun was out, she'd sit in the backyard to work on the tan she'd lost.

Every couple of days, Gramma would call to see how she was doing. "Hi, Tara! How are you?" she would ask. "How is your arm now? Your mom said the doctor might have to break it again so that it heals right."

"Well, I guess they're worried that I won't be able rotate my wrist once my arm's done healing, and they told Mom that they should break it and reset it to make sure I get what they call a 'full range of motion.' Mom is worried about my wrist, but she said that she was more worried about everything I've gone through and so she'd rather wait to see how it heals before deciding to break it all over again."

"My Lord! How will you go to camp with a broken arm in a cast?"

"That's just the thing. They think that by the time I go to camp I can have some sort of half cast, and then I'll just wrap it with a tensor bandage. Then, when I want to go swimming and stuff, I can just unwrap it so it will be OK if I get my arm wet."

"Well, that's good, dear. I'm so glad you can go. I was hoping that something else would happen this summer, something good, because I just don't think I can cope with any more trouble."

"Here's something good, Gramma. I asked Mom if I could come and visit you next week, and she said I could! Would you like that?"

"Oh, boy, would I ever! I'll tell all my friends that my granddaughter Tara is coming to see me, and that she's coming along just fine since her accident. 'She's pretty perky,' I'll tell them, and that, sooner than later, she'll be fit as a fiddle."

"OK! I love you, Gramma. See you soon!"

Tara smiled as she hung up the phone.

———————◆━◁◯▷━◆———————

It was late Saturday afternoon and Tara had just been dropped off at home after spending a few days visiting her stepdad. He had reminded her that her mom had gone out for the day, so once she got in the house, she put her overnight bag in her room, checked on the pets, and headed to the kitchen. On the counter by the telephone, she found a note from her mom. She said she'd left that morning to go on a hike with a new group of people she'd become friends with.

Tara was just putting the kettle on when her mom walked in the kitchen door.

"Oh, hi little girl. I'm happy you're home!" she said as she took off her hiking boots and washed her hands in the sink. "How was your time away?"

"Hey Mom!" Tara gave her a hug and grabbed another teacup from the cupboard.

"I was busy trying to keep the dog out of the chicken coop most of the time, but it was fun. How was your hike?"

"Oh, Tara. It was the most wonderful day! We walked all the way from the town of Harmony to Wildwood Park," she said as she sat down at the kitchen table with her tea. "I didn't know what to expect—I'd never walked more than two miles before—but the weather was perfect and there were no clouds and there was a lovely breeze, *and* I was able to keep up with the rest of the group.

"We walked through every kind of terrain: hills, corn fields, tall grasses, wooded areas. It was just like Heaven. I couldn't take the smile off my face. Mostly we walked in single file, so although I was with other people I felt alone, but not lonely. And you know what? I've never felt so at peace."

She took a sip of her tea. "I started thinking about my life, and about all the people that care about me, and I realized that I am truly lucky that my kids, my family, and my friends all love me. But, even with all this love, I kept asking myself why I've never felt happy."

She put her cup down and took Tara's hand. "Since you were in that accident, Tara, I began to analyze myself and I realized how close I came to being truly unhappy. Unhappy wouldn't even be near the right word if something happened to you. Imagine if I'd lost you?" Her voice cracked and her eyes welled up with tears. She squeezed Tara's hand, then she cleared her throat and continued.

"I know that I need to let go of Mrs. Wrenn and all the sadness of my childhood. And that's what I'm going to work on while you're at Gramma's next week. But I have to tell you, I've been thinking about you all day, little girl."

Tara adjusted herself in her seat, interested in what her mom had to say.

"You are growing up so fast. It just seems like yesterday that you were my baby, the little girl that used to follow me around the house, talking and talking and telling me about your day. You've always been so happy-go-lucky and I admire that about you. The way you love your life, your family, and school. The passion you have for dancing and singing and playing outside with your friends. It all makes me so happy." She pushed her cold teacup aside. "But, sometimes Tara, it makes me feel a little bit sad."

"Why does that make you feel sad?" Tara worried when her mom felt sad.

Her mom smiled gently and said, "When I see you dancing through life, with no cares in the world and nothing to worry about, I wonder what that feels like. I didn't have a childhood like yours and I think sometimes I feel a bit jealous...or maybe envious, is a better word. And I wonder if because of that you've felt uncomfortable telling me about how much Gramma loves you and about how much fun you have with her."

Tara realized she had always felt a little guilty telling her mom about her relationship with Gramma, but she didn't think her mom had noticed.

"Because that's the last thing I want. I want everyone to love you and I want you to be happy and carefree. I would hate for you to feel the way I felt when I was little, and so I want to apologize to you if I've ever made you feel bad."

Tara could feel tears welling up in her eyes but couldn't blink them away.

Her mom stood up and pulled her into her arms.

"You're my little girl, Tara, and I will make sure that you never feel responsible for me and Gramma again. It's not your job to fix us, and I want you to stop worrying about it and just concentrate on your own little life."

Tara let herself sink into her mom's arms. She hadn't realized until now that she had been holding on, almost as if holding her breath, whenever she was with her mom and grandmother at the same time. She desperately wanted them to love each other, but she felt relieved now that her mom was telling her not to worry so much.

"I just love you both so much," Tara said, her face buried in her mom's neck.

"I know, and we love you too, little girl. Everything's going to be just fine."

Tara didn't know how her mom was going to make everything OK, but for the first time, she finally had hope.

CHAPTER NINETEEN

Late Summer 1984—Goodbye Little Girl

On Sunday morning the following week, Tara woke up in Gramma's living room to a warm, sunny day. She'd slept in because her mom wasn't coming until late afternoon to pick her up and take her back home to Kitchener.

While she laid there, she listened for the familiar sounds of the house. Big Joe didn't have to go to work because he'd retired from St. Mary's Cement a few weeks ago, so Tara figured he was already out in his garden. And Joey must have left already to go to the restaurant because he'd said he had to open for the manager.

She relaxed on the couch listening to see what Gramma might be up to, when she heard her on the phone in the front hall. After a few minutes, she realized that Gramma was talking to her brother, Doug.

"Well, I must say that today is a beautiful day, Doug. Yup, Tara has been with me since last Sunday. I said last Sunday! Cathy brought her down as she wanted to come to be with me. Yes, I know, she is lucky she's alive after what she went through.

It's like a miracle. I know…God only knows. Anyway, she's been enjoying herself with me. I said she's been enjoying herself! No, we can't go to Mass today because Cathy's coming. I said, Cathy's coming. Oh my Lord, Doug, I have to go. Yup, we'll talk to ya later. 'Bye."

Tara knew that her great-uncle Doug was hard of hearing, and it drove Gramma nuts having to repeat herself all the time.

"My God, that man can't hear a bloody thing and it's getting on my nerves. I wish he'd go to the doctor and get those ears checked," Gramma said as she came into the living room. "Anyway, good morning, dear. How'd you sleep?"

"Real good, Gramma. I guess Big Joe's outside?"

"Yes he is. That's what he's been doing every morning since he retired. You know, I might as well get used to the idea of having him around for a while; it sure will be different for me, being as I'm used to being at home by myself. Oh well, I guess everything will work out fine." She shrugged. "Did I tell you that we went to a country BBQ last week? Oh, it was a grand time. They had more food than you can imagine, and drinks and desserts and music, and when it got dark they lit a bonfire and, oh, was it ever a beautiful time! Joe and I have never done anything like that before, so I guess it's good that he's retired. He sure seems a lot more relaxed than before."

Tara smiled listening to Gramma, but she wondered if Gramma *was* happy to have Big Joe home all day, every day. Tara knew Gramma liked having her time during the day to watch her soaps and relax in her chair.

"Alright, dear," Gramma said, interrupting her thoughts. "It's Sunday and it's time for me to spray the Lysol. I know you hate the smell, so why don't you run up and wash your teeth and get dressed while I spray the house down."

Tara pulled back the blankets and was careful getting off the couch. She still didn't trust her legs one hundred per cent, but they seemed to be getting stronger every day and they carried her up the stairs to the bathroom. After she was done brushing her teeth and flushing the darned toilet, she was about to go back down the stairs but instead, she glanced into Nana's gloomy bedroom.

She went straight to the window and opened the curtains to let the sunshine in. The white-painted room was now bathed in sunlight, so bright it almost hurt her eyes. Once her eyes adjusted, Tara looked around the familiar room and wasn't surprised to see that nothing had really changed. There was Nana's bed with her blankets still tucked under the mattress, the crucifix still hung above the headboard, and on her tri-fold mirror dresser were her hairbrush and handheld mirror. Tara's eyes welled up when she saw that mirror. She could picture Nana on one of her silly days, saying, "Oh Lord, would you look at that," and then rolling her eyes to the heavens and shaking her head.

So much had happened since Nana died back in March, but Tara still couldn't get over the fact that she'd never see her again. She realized now just how much she'd loved her great-grandmother, and she counted herself lucky that she'd got to spend so much time with her. She would never forget their special bond, and she would remember her every day in her prayers.

Before she turned away, Tara tiptoed over to the dresser and carefully pulled open the drawer. She pushed away some of the items that were still there, and under an old prayer book she found what she was looking for: a few Scotch mints. She touched them lightly, smiling at her memories of Nana and blinking back tears. Then she gently shut the drawer, leaving the mints alone and safe inside their tissue.

She left Nana's bedroom door wide open to brighten the dim hallway and made her way slowly and quietly down the stairs. She knew now that there were no monsters in the attic room, and smiled thinking about how she used to race down the stairs to try to get away from them. She said hello to the African Violets and checked herself out in the mirror. She was pretty skinny looking, that was for sure. Her knees looked knobby and her elbows were pointy. The scar on her face was bright red, but the doctors told her that eventually it would fade. She had a thing in her mouth that they called a *partial*, and they'd set five fake teeth in it. It had been uncomfortable at first, but she was getting used to it now and was happy with her smile.

"C'mon, Tara, your breakfast is getting cold," Gramma said, calling from the kitchen.

Later that afternoon, they were sitting in the living room with their tea, watching television when Tara's mom came in the front door.

"Hello!" she said, calling out as she walked into the living room.

Tara was surprised to see that her mom was smiling and her lips weren't pressed tightly together like they normally were when she came to Gramma's house.

"How are you two doing?" she asked, throwing her purse on the couch.

"Hi, hun. You look like you got some sun," Gramma said, getting up from her chair and heading toward the kitchen. "You sit down and relax and I'll get you a cup of tea."

"Thanks, Mom," she said as she went over to hug Tara. "Hello, little girl, how are you feeling?"

After Tara let her mom know she was feeling fine, Gramma came back in with the tea and sat down in her chair. Her mom settled herself at the end of the couch and smiled behind her teacup. Finally, she said, "I have some wonderful news to tell you."

Tara scooched to the edge of the couch. "What, Mom? What wonderful news?"

"Well, I'm going to start by telling you both," she inhaled deeply and let it out slowly, "that I'm changing my name."

Gramma and Tara blinked, not knowing what to say.

"I will no longer be Cathy. From now on, and for the rest of my life, I am going to be Catherine. Catherine Barron."

Her mother beamed as she took a quick sip of her tea. "It all started last Saturday, when I decided to go on a hike with this group I found. When I got home, I told Tara all about it and after she went to bed that night, I decided to start a journal to see if I could use the peace I'd found during the hike to reflect on my life and get to the root of my unhappiness. Before writing down my thoughts I wanted to write down my name, but then I paused. I had an overwhelming feeling at that moment that I needed to make a decision about who I was, and what my name was going to be. It was clear to me that, somehow, my name was connected to my childhood; the reason why I've felt so unhappy all these years.

"And then, yesterday, I went to Grand Bend beach. It was a perfect day. There was a constant wind that reminded me of the cool breeze from the Atlantic Ocean on a warm day in Cape Breton. I walked and walked, and when I got hot I went in the water—not far, just to my waist. I was on the beach for hours, thanking God that you'd survived that fall, Tara, but also thinking about how to let go of my childhood.

"Then, last night I went back to the journal and wrote, 'My name is Catherine Barron. But before I can be Catherine Barron, I have to write the story of a woman named Mrs. Wrenn who ruined my childhood.' I wrote for hours. I didn't stop until I'd written down every little thing she'd done to make my life miserable. And slowly, after a while, I felt calmer, lighter, and just like during the hike, full of peace.

"So I've decided to let go of Cathy, the sad, hurt little girl that I have been protecting, and I'm going to be Catherine. A woman who's taking control of her life, letting the past be the past, and looking forward to being the happy person that she wants to be."

She turned to Gramma. "Mom, I realized something else when I was writing last night. I have spent my whole life resenting Mrs. Wrenn. Because of her, I've always felt stupid and unloved, and with that came frustration and disappointment about everything in my life. I've always been mad at her for the way she treated me, but you know what?" Her mom took a deep breath.

"I think I finally understand, Mom, that I'm actually very mad at you. I think that all the anger I've kept for Mrs. Wrenn really should have been aimed at you."

Gramma's hands started shaking but she kept them clasped together in her lap.

Her mom took another deep breath and shifted to the edge of the couch. "I'm angry at you for taking me away from Nana and making me live with Mrs. Wrenn. I'm mad at you for not listening to me or believing me when I told you how mean she was. And I'm upset at you for not sticking up for me when I needed you to." Her mom's voice got higher, as if her chest was tightening. "But I think what breaks my heart the most is that you never said you were sorry. You never acknowledged how hurt I was. You just dismissed my feelings and made me feel like I didn't matter. As a child, I didn't want to believe that you weren't a good mother. I wanted to love you, I wanted to be proud of you, but I was disappointed that you didn't act like the mother I wanted."

Visibly fighting back tears, her mom continued. "I spent my whole life not wanting to admit that to myself, so I just blamed Mrs. Wrenn instead of you. It was easier being mad at her because she wouldn't be able to fix anything. I was sinking into this unhappy place that eventually became more comfortable than knowing that you'd never say you're sorry."

She closed her eyes for a moment, but when she spoke again her voice was calm. "All my life I've felt like there was a shadow haunting me, and the shadow wouldn't allow me to feel happiness. I used to think that the shadow was Mrs. Wrenn, but I now know, Mom, that all along my shadow was you."

Gramma tried to interrupt. "Cathy, I—"

"Wait, before you say anything. I want you to know that I think you are a loving person. I see it when you're with Tara, and even though I don't feel it from you it's not because you don't want to be that person for me. It's because I won't let you. I've always tried to protect myself from my disappointment in you, but I know now that I have to let you in.

"I read something recently about a Rebecca Wells book and it makes so much sense: 'A mother–daughter love can be an imperfect love, and forgiveness, more than understanding, is what is needed.' So, Mom, I'm going to say that I may not understand you, but I forgive you."

Tara closed her eyes, having no idea what was going to happen next, but she hoped against all hope that Gramma would do what she knew her mom longed for.

She opened her eyes and saw Gramma get out of her chair and walk over to her daughter.

Gramma reached out and placed her hands on her daughter's shoulders. "I love you, Catherine. I'm sorry for everything that I did and didn't do. I don't want to be your shadow—I want to be your mother."

At first her mom froze, but then she stood up and allowed Gramma to take her in her arms. Tears slowly rolled down Gramma's cheeks, and Tara smiled when she saw through her own tears, that her mom was smiling too.

After Gramma and Mom had dried their tears and given each other another hug, Tara's mom said she wanted to go up to the bathroom to wash her face. Gramma went into the kitchen to put the kettle on again, and Tara sat on the couch and wondered what it would be like from now on. What would it be like for Mom and Gramma to finally have a nice relationship?

Since she was five years old, Tara had known that her mom was angry with Mrs. Wrenn. Then, when she'd got a little older, she realized that her mom was hurt too. Hurt by Gramma and what Gramma had and hadn't done. Tara had hoped that, by talking to her mom and talking to Gramma, she could somehow bring them together. That they would say they were sorry and forgive and forget. But, try as she might, Tara hadn't been able to do that for them so she'd given up. Little did she know, that by going into the forest to play with her friend Jenny one day, she'd end up in the hospital. Had her accident brought her mom and Gramma closer together? Did almost losing her make them both take a step back and realize how precious and fragile life is?

Tara hoped that they would have forgiven each other without her accident, but if there was a silver lining, something to be positive about, it was that they'd had this opportunity to move on and be happy.

Tara breathed a sigh of relief. No matter how it had happened, whether her accident had anything to do with it or not, her heart was full of love for her mom and her grandmother, because now she knew they loved each other too.

After a few minutes Tara realized that her mom was taking a long time upstairs, so she went up to see if she was OK. Her mom wasn't in the bathroom or in Nana's room, where Tara suspected she'd go, so she made her way down the short hallway, and found her in Gramma's room.

She was sitting at the old dresser, gazing at herself in the mirror.

"Are you alright, Mom?" Tara sat on the bed, looking at her mother's image in the mirror.

"You know, Tara," she said, not looking away from her reflection. "When I was your age, my best friend was the little girl in the mirror. I used to think that she was taking care of me by letting me talk to her and tell her my secrets. But, now...I realize that *I* was the one taking care of *her*." She smiled faintly at her mirrored image. "I was trying to console the little girl and tell her that everything would be alright, but it seemed like nothing I said made her feel better. I carried her sadness around with me my whole life. But, I understand now that I want to be happy and the only way I can do that is by letting her go. I need to say goodbye to the sad little girl from so long ago. I need to wrap her up in a warm blanket, brush her hair back from her forehead, touch her cheek, and say goodbye."

She reached out and softly touched the reflection with her fingertips.

"Goodbye, Cathy."

Then she took her daughter's hand and led her into the hallway warmed by the sunlight streaming in from Nana's room.

Smiling at Tara, she gently closed the bedroom door.

AUTHOR'S NOTE

"Gramma died of pneumonia in 2006,
when she was eighty-two years old.

My mom, Catherine, died of cancer in 2010,
when she was sixty years old.

I am a forty eight year-old woman who is happily married
with two beautiful daughters.

I wrote this story for them...for all of them."

—Tara Schippling Mondou

Nana, Gramma, Cathy, Tara

Photos

Gramma's Porch Summer 1977

Tara Cathy Nana Gramma 1978

Tara in Kitchener 1978

One of Nana's perms

Tara in Kitchener 1978

Cape Breton outside Big Molly's house

Joey and Gramma in front of the pantry 1970

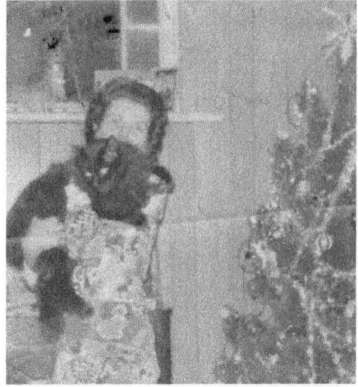
Gramma and Smokey Christmas 1972

Gramma and kids she babysat

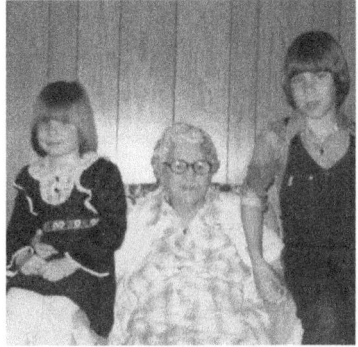
Tara Nana Ronnie 1978

Tara modeling in 1979

Tara dancing in 1979

Cathy and Tara in Kitchener 1979

Cathy and Big Joe

Cathy and Joey

Nana being silly

Tara grade 3

Cathy

Gramma with Ginger and friend

Nana with her mirror and heating pad

Nana saying Oh Lord

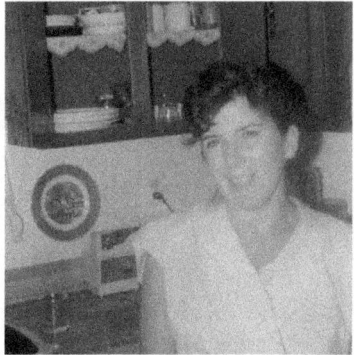

Cathy in Kitchener

Tara and Nana

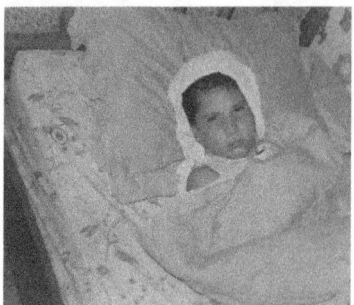

Tara at home with Sisters of the Precious Blood

Ronnie Marlene Wendell Tara

Cathy at Gramma's table

Tara the Wild Child at the Barn

Gramma Ginger Cathy near the railway tracks

Cathy Nana Marlene when Nana's sick

Cathy and Tara First Holy Communion
1984

Tara and Gramma First Holy Communion
1984

Tree chopped after girl seriously hurt in fall

Firemen fault tree-house 12 metres aloft in bush

By Dianne Wood
Record staff

A tree containing a child's tree-house was chopped down today following an accident Monday that left a 10-year-old girl in serious condition in hospital.

Tara Schippling of 574 Strasburg Rd., Kitchener, fell out of the tree-house in a wooded area behind her home after swinging on a branch about 12 metres (40 feet) above the ground, Kitchener fire department capt. Ed Stahley said Monday.

A spokesman with the Waterloo region roads maintenance department said the tree was cut down at the request of Waterloo regional police. The tree was on regional property backing on the old Kitchener landfill site.

She is in serious condition in the intensive care unit at St. Mary's Hospital with a broken left wrist and facial cuts, a hospital spokesman said Monday. The spokesman said it was too soon to tell whether she had more serious injuries, but that she was being watched closely.

Later Monday night her mother, Kathy Edwards, said Tara also suffered a punctured lung and will require some plastic surgery to her face. Hospital officials planned to operate today on her face and arm.

She said they wanted to watch her overnight to ensure she had no head injuries.

"She's getting better," Edwards said after spending most of the evening at the hospital. "I'm so glad

"I'm recommending to Waterloo regional police and to the fire prevention people to have it removed," Stahley said of the tree-house. 15 metres (50 feet) above the ground

Jenny Mueller, one of Tara's friends, said the tree-house was built by a neighborhood boy. Wooden rungs nailed on to the trunk providing access

Stahley said that while he was investigating the accident, a neighborhood girl who appeared to be about six years old told him she had once been injured in climbing in the tree

know the tree-house existed.

"I hadn't gone back there. I didn't know there was an actual house. I knew they played on trees."

Maintenance workers from Waterloo Region chop a tree into pieces after a 10-year-old girl fell from a tree-house.
Philip Walker, Record staff

Girl Falls out of a Tree 1984

Tara Mondou

AUTHOR

Growing up, Tara fell in love with the stories she was told about her mother, grandmother and great grandmother. As the women she loved passed away, she knew she had to keep their memories alive for her own daughters, by putting pen to paper and writing their stories.

In 2016, Tara Mondou published her first novel, *"Little Girl in the Mirror, Cathy's Story"*.

In 2022, she published the companion novel, *"Me and My Shadow, Tara's Story"*.

Tara co-founded a writers' support group called Cambridge Authors; was the 2018 recipient of the Bernice Adams Memorial Award for Communication/Literary Arts; volunteers as the Public Relations Director for Guitars for Kids Waterloo Region, and is the Chair of the Board at the Waterloo Regional Block Parent® Program.

Tara often travels back to Cape Breton where it all began. She is fascinated by her family history, and while walking the windy cliffs high above the Atlantic Ocean, finds inspiration to write her next book.

Tara lives in the historic West Galt area of Cambridge, Ontario with her husband and their two daughters.

CPSIA information can be obtained
at www.ICGtesting.com
Printed in the USA
BVHW042204151122
652066BV00003B/13